Scatterlogical Wisdom

A MEMOIR

BY
FRANCES HALL

Published by Frances Hall, in association with Wild Side Publishing
PO Box 33, Ruawai 0549, New Zealand www.wildsidepublishing.com

Cover design & text layout, Janet Curle | wildsidepublishing.com
Owl icons inside the text (except the cover owl) are designed by Finn Jackson

Family Tree: **Grandparents,** Ernest and Elizabeth Brickell
 Parents, Stan and Thelma Hall
 Siblings, Robin, Juliet, Richard and Peter
 Children, Tracey, Amanda, Richard and Emily
 Grandchildren, Jazz, Finn, Amelia, Chelsea, Isabella,
 Georgia, Christian, Ava and Ezra

Cataloguing in Publication Data:
Title: Scatterlogical Wisdom

ISBN: 978-0-473-51592-8 (pbk)
ISBN: 978-0-473-51593-5 (ebook)

Subjects: Inspiration, Spirituality, Body Soul Spirit, Christian, Non-Fiction, New Zealand, Memoir, Travel

First New Zealand printing, March 2020, Blue Star bluestar.co.nz

International listing, Ingram Spark, March 2020 via wildsidepublishing.com

Dedication

To Mum,

This is the book you never got to write.

Frances xox

Endorsements

"*Never a dull moment!* Those words must've been spoken over Frances Hall the day she was born. Because, in a world littered with well-meaning people who bore their friends to death, Frances has always done the exact opposite. Especially to those of us who've wandered the road with her. Full of fun, and sometimes mad as a meat-axe, she's made the most of an overflowing (and by no means easy-peasy) life. And, along the way, she's collected insights that have often stopped me in my tracks: *'Did she really say that?'* This book's a keeper, Frances. Your memoirs will delight and inspire. So what's next?"
-**John Cooney, publisher** *Grapevine Magazine*

"Scatterlogical Wisdom is a delight to read. Frances Hall has written about her life with humour and grace, in a way that embraces how messy and unpredictable real-life can be. With a thirst for travel and adventure, through good times and challenging times, this down-to-earth memoir is scattered with pearls of wisdom that will resonate with many readers."
-**Karen McMillan, author** of *Unbreakable Spirit, Brushstrokes of Memory* and the *Elastic Island Adventure* series

"A brilliantly written, insightful and hysterically funny memoir— with hidden depth. A great read for those wanting to find the way to laugh at the hard times and see sense in the nonsense. You will accidentally stumble upon real nuggets of wisdom in the process of tracking one amazing woman's journey."
-**Janet Balcombe, author** *The Wild Side* and *Radical Lives 1 & 2*

Contents

Introduction

Wisdom shouts in the streets.
She cries out in the public square. She calls to the crowds
along the main street,
to those gathered in front of the city gate:
"How long, you simpletons,
 will you insist on being simple-minded?"

Proverbs 1:20-33

Wisdom and I are strange bedfellows. Although I need her every single day, I don't want to suffer to get her. I'd like her to turn up in a bed of roses.

Wise people make me nervous. When I'm around them I tend to open my mouth and over-vent. They listen patiently to my ranting, wait until both my feet are so firmly in my mouth that I'm gagging, and then drop a pearl of wisdom so profound that I completely miss the point.

I must be extra polite to wise people because I don't want to upset them by admitting I have no idea what they're talking about.

Wise people don't write books like this because that wouldn't be wise.

This is the reason this book has been five years in the writing. The difficult times can only be processed in hindsight, after the white-hot pain has subsided and I have some healed perspective.

As Alice Steinbach says, "...a lot happened—but I was too deeply engaged in the experience to observe it as a writer. It was the writer's classic dilemma, to let the observing-self take charge, or to give the upper hand to the deeper-experiencing-self."

So why am I writing this?

Because my thirst for wisdom, knowledge, and understanding has never been satisfied; because I know I'm not wise; because falling on my face has taught me how to stand on my feet. And I believe I share with you the struggle to rise above your circumstances while keeping your feet on the ground.

Even if all you do is laugh at my stupidity until you're incontinent or your ribs ache, I'll know that my job is done.

And so, let's leap off the cliff of stupidity and hope and pray wisdom opens our parachutes just in time.

My life has been an attempt to make sense of wisdom. In hindsight, I was always only going to learn from my mistakes, not from the wise words of history.

Later in my life, I wrote short radio scripts. I read them now and realise they were an account of my life's experiences.

In this book I'll attempt to tie them together and hopefully inspire others to tell their story and prevail.

1

The meaning of life

I recall when it all started. As a young child, the middle one of five, I had an undeniable longing for a life destined, a life with meaning and purpose, a life more travelled. I woke up every morning believing something amazing was going to happen. It rarely did.

I wanted to be me and all that meant. I didn't want to leave anything unsaid, undone, or unseen, or unthought. Trouble in the making, I was never a dreamy kid, more of a visionary. Life was something to be lassoed, wrangled and corralled.

I'd also inherited my mother's tendency to what she called "the thinkies". These came at all hours of the day and night—ideas, concepts, troubleshooting, problem-solving, possibility-thinking—long before it all became popular. As I rode the school bus from the farm into high school, my visionary-self took flight. I could be a famous actress or a singer—or anything else. I would be discovered—I just wasn't sure what I'd be doing at the time.

Again, I attribute this to Mum. She would visit the local library and come home with the car full of an eclectic pile of glorious books, which opened my world to the thoughts, feelings, and cultures of a huge universe. I absorbed these like a sponge.

A country girl with precocious tendencies was never going to be most popular and I learned early on that my walk could be quite a lonely one until I had assembled my adoring audience. I'm still waiting.

My Mum told me that once I stood up on a chair in the audience at a school concert and belted out the rest of a song when another child struck with stage fright forgot the words. A modest involvement in musical theatre was birthed that day.

Even as a young child I had yearnings and longings for a different life. An innate knowledge that your life means something and is hovering to be born is well-summed up in the words of Sally Field. She described her emerging talent as "Fireflies on the edges of my eyes". I would later discover the sheer joy of doing what I'm gifted to do.

I picked up on the emotional vibes around me and constantly felt the need to make sense of them. I instinctively knew that I carried the mental and emotional genes of those before me.

To a certain extent I was doomed to aspiration because derring-do preceded me...

The chair

The rocking chair in the corner of my lounge is adorned with a modern, bright aqua, chevron-patterned cushion. The streaming morning sun highlights its vintage—it's at least a hundred years old. My dad treated it for borer; the latticed rattan seat was restored, and then re-varnished.

One morning I sat and rocked and remembered the love story passed through three generations.

My grandfather fought at Gallipoli and in the French trenches. Glorious it was not. 'Hellish' is a better description. But at least one good thing came out of the war for him.

As he and his fellow Kiwis battled, a group of young Scottish women met in Dundee to knit warm hats and socks for the soldiers. They then packed bullets in boxes together with the items they'd knitted. Some wrote little notes of encouragement and, as in my grandma's case, included their names and addresses.

Little did she know that, one day, when he was granted R-and-R leave, a young Kiwi soldier, Ernest Burdett Brickell of the Wellington Infantry Battalion, would make his way by train along the length of England and Scotland and turn up on her doorstep.

A wartime romance blossomed. My grandmother, Elizabeth, came to New Zealand in 1919 and the family settled in the Wairarapa.

The chair tells the story of their lives together; of two children, rocked and fed and soothed. Maybe, my grandma rocked and soothed herself as she settled in this strange land away from her family. I'm sure she cried in this chair and I can also hear laughter and the lovely lilt of her Scottish accent as she chatted with friends over a cup of tea.

I remember her gnarled hands resting lightly on the lovingly carved arms of this antique chair, as she stared ahead, reminiscing her ninety years of life.

The rocking chair may seem a bit incongruous in my ultra-modern apartment, surrounded by leather and chrome, but it reminds me of this gutsy little Scottish lassie, and that if she had not travelled to a faraway land, I wouldn't be here at all.

We owe so much to these brave men and women. New Zealand's population was less than two million then and we lost nearly 30,000 lives over both wars.

As I reflect on their sacrifice, I pen the next stories...

3

Anzacs

A few years ago, while on his OE, my son, Richard, visited Gallipoli on Anzac Day to pay his respects to his great-grandfather who served there, to gain an understanding of the huge sacrifice so many New Zealanders made.

It looked so impossible, so against the odds, so bleak and dangerous. Yet our men fought bravely, never giving up until they could battle no more.

He took a photo of the famous plaque erected by the Turks: "Those heroes that shed their blood and lost their lives .... You now lie in the soil of a friendly country. Therefore, rest in peace. There is no difference between the Johnnies and the Mehmets to us, where they lie side by side here in this country of ours ... you, the mothers, who sent their sons from far away countries, wipe away your tears; your sons are now lying in our bosom and are in peace. After having lost their lives on this land they have become our sons as well."

I looked through his other photos, and found one of him sleeping peacefully, waiting for the dawn service to start and it hit me that, in a different era, it could have been him lying dead on a foreign battlefield.

Lest we forget.

In the day-to-dayness of life, I found I was often laid low by the turning up of an unexpected drama. Who would've thought that could happen to a mother of four...cue sarcasm. It was often hard to find silver linings in clouds or even the existence of daylight, but they were there...

Flying High

My Dad, Stan, was a pilot in WWII. He died many years ago but with Anzac Day approaching I think about him and the price he paid to defend New Zealand.

After the war he still longed to fly and eventually became a gliding instructor. It must have been a far cry from flying hospital planes and being shot at above the jungles of Burma. He often talked about the peace he found when soaring through the sky. He used to go on about cloud formations and the need for a good thermal pattern to keep the glider aloft. These thermals give the plane "lift" and keep it from ending up in a farmer's backyard miles from the airfield.

Dad took me for a flight one day. I then understood what he was talking about and I've learned to apply the search for "lift" to my own life on terra firma.

Sometimes I find it in a kind word from a friend, sometimes in seeing a beautiful flower or a sunset. And in moments of crisis I find it in the words, "God help me!"

I've learned it comes from looking up, from being grateful, from helping others. When my children went to Sunday School, they learned lovely little songs that reflected their childlike faith.

One of them contained the words "If you want joy, then jump for it" and this line was repeated three times. Sometimes I need to fly through turbulence or do joy-jumping to get the lift I need.

So, here's to you Dad. I want you to know I'm still finding the wind beneath my wings.

I cannot begin to imagine the conditions under which Dad had to function. I guess it was the Kiwi humour that got him through, as the troops managed to have a laugh in the midst of very trying times.

Wolf in Monkey Clothing

After a year in England, Dad and his RNZAF squadron, number 238, were posted to Burma. The RAF flew them to India. They then faced a five-day train trip to their Burmese base. The train was pretty basic with wooden benches for seats, and the trip was tedious. They lived, slept and ate in the carriages.

Early in the trip, a large, friendly monkey jumped onto their train. They named him "George" and petted him and fed him from their rations. As they moved further north and it became colder, they cut down an old jacket and made George a little tunic, complete with Air Force insignia, to stop him shivering.

After a few days they pulled into a proper station with a large tank overflowing with the water which was used to cool the engines.

The men stripped off, had a welcome shower, then went inside the station for a leisurely meal.

After a while they heard a noisy commotion and went out to investigate. The train was surrounded by scores of Indian men, women and children, and George was passing through the windows all the men's belongings from their kit bags.

George was unceremoniously tossed off the train.

In New Zealand, Mum and Dad set about building their lives together. Dad would rather have been flying than milking cows, but this was what he had to do so that was what he did. Every time a small plane flew over the farm, Dad would rush outside and gaze longingly into the sky. Later he was able to fly a small plane himself. He would fly over our house and tip the wings from side to side to say hello.

4

My Mother

My heart reaches into the past which subconsciously im-
printed my DNA with the effects of two world wars and
a depression. I felt Dad's need to be frugal and Mum's need to
spread her intellectual wings. As I grew older, I began to appreciate her and had the privilege of getting to know her as my
friend and confidante.

When I was a child, my mother was like a 24-hour conveni-
ence store, always open and a source of everything I needed.
When I was a teenager, she was the barrier between me and
a dodgy social life. Then as an adult, and a mother, I began to
understand what a huge job she had, raising five children and
staying sane. As she aged, our roles changed, and I became like
her sister and then like her parent in her fading years. I loved
the sister role best, hanging out in coffee shops and giggling
about sex.

I confessed that I'd found her Dutch cap in her wardrobe
one day and wondered what it was for. At the time I thought it
may be part of a toilet plunger but couldn't understand why it
was hidden in the closet.

I held an uncanny sense of responsibility for any tension in our household and developed a sophisticated sense of humour to jolly everybody along. I felt that all problems could be solved by more effort, more ideas, more determination, and more fun.

I asked Dad for 20c to go to a school play and when he said he didn't have it I went on a scavenger hunt. I left no cushion unturned, no nook or cranny unsearched, and I found that money.

When I was born, New Zealand as a nation was barely one hundred years old. Embedded in our psyche was a pioneering can-do attitude. I was crowned runner-up to Miss Whangarei City in a cute little white dress I'd sewn up a few days before the final. We all stitched and baked and dug - a basic but well-grounded upbringing. The wooden spoon ruled, and not just to stir the gravy. I might add that this spoon was not made from lightweight bamboo, it was a force to be reckoned with.

The many high spots included owning my own pony and competing at the Whangarei AMP shows. We rode to a local pony club run by two farming spinsters who allegedly tied their demented mother to a chair in the cowshed while they milked the cows. Our community held a vast array of eccentric people! My first seven years of education were in a two-roomed school where our valiant teacher taught six grades at once. Amazingly, the principal of the school provided extra learning materials for me so I wouldn't get bored.

I tasted my first terror and my first bravery at the school dental clinic, unaffectionately named "The Murder House" by its young visitors. Every dental nurse was well trained in the art of torture. No anaesthetic was used and we learned to literally grin and bear the drilling. Breaking down in front of your classmates and admitting you were terrified was not a viable option.

Nor did it get you out of going to the dentist.

On rare occasions, Mum and Dad went out for an evening and left me and my teenage sister home alone. We lived in the country, which is not the quiet, peaceful place you would imagine. All sorts of strange noises manifest themselves in the dark. Animals snort and snuffle and moo and neigh. As kids, we could identify most of them but any noise out-of-the-ordinary scared us witless.

We would pretend to be Mum and Dad, lowering our voices and saying scary things like, "Just as well we keep that gun under the bed. Those shooting lessons could be handy if anyone breaks in."

We desperately needed to inform potential criminals that someone "big" was in the house. It obviously worked; we were never attacked.

Farming

As a teenager, the whole farming thing gave me the creeps. From my experience, removing the smell of cow muck from one's person is very difficult. When a "townie" boy wanted to take me on a date, there was no way I'd want to turn up reeking of cow doodoo. There were no showers in our house, just a bathtub with the water shared by at least two people. (I can understand where the saying came, "Be careful not to throw the baby out with the bathwater.")

I was thrilled when I could leave home and join the 'madding crowds' in town, reveling in the taste of "real" milk rather than the thick, creamy stuff straight from the cow. I've since lived overseas, travelled extensively, and stayed firmly urban. But every now and again those skills I learned on the farm have come in handy.

Behind our house, we had a large, paved courtyard which, in torrential downpours tended to retain water. When the rain stopped, I'd get out there with the broom.

Sweeping quantities of liquid from a solid surface was part of my education in the cowshed. Although rainwater is slightly different in texture to bovine effluent, the technique remains the same. Sweep strongly and vigorously in one direction and follow that with several quick brush strokes to make sure the water doesn't return. I found this chore strangely invigorating. This just goes to show—"you can take the girl out of the country, but you can't take the country out of the girl".

When drought hit the farm, the cows went dry early. I remember dragging the garden hose to the fence to water the paddocks so that the grass would grow, one of my early attempts at problem-solving on a large scale.

And yet, a country upbringing is somewhat feral. Other than the usual nods to routine, the rest of the time is unfettered. Reading became my favourite pastime. I read everything I could find, even books on animal husbandry—which were a bit of an eye-opener.

Reading gives way to dreaming and the future spreads out like an expansive garden waiting to be harvested.

I sensed early on that my mum was an intellectual giant. She cooked and cleaned for five children, but her passion lay in the use of words. When hot water was plentiful, we had "lashings" of it. We were instructed not to "wolf" our food when a simple "eat slowly" sufficed.

Her love of words engendered in all five of us the need to be literate and to express ourselves well. She hated foul language and thought people that used it lacked intelligence. I still cannot let out an expletive without sensing her disapproval. If we asked about a word, she would tell us to look it up in the dictionary. I still feel a frisson of delight every time I open a thesaurus.

Although I never had an elocution lesson like the "townie" children had, I entered local speech competitions and won prizes, just because I could.

Mum was the ultimate positivist—like Norman Vincent Peale on steroids. She could forgive anybody almost anything. Even Texas axe murderers were redeemable if they showed signs of intelligence or had excellent axe-sharpening skills. But she could also be scathing about "drongos"—people who complained about their lot in life but never tried to improve things.

She believed all her children were exceptional and woe betide anyone who indicated otherwise. (It was a shock to learn later in life that I was not God's gift to mankind.)

Mum also taught us the skills of good conversation, with tips like these...

Foot in Mouth Disease

Think before you speak and make sure your words are useful and life-giving. Don't rabbit on for ages about boring details unless there is another boring-detail person there. They deserve to suffer.

Do suffer fools gladly and keep smiling as you leave—quickly if possible. (Note to self. Answering before listening is both stupid and rude.)

Although I am much more interesting than anybody else, the world at large may not have caught up with that revelation. So, with my two ears and my one mouth, listen, listen, then talk.

Be wary of people who start a conversation with the words, "It's really interesting...". It usually isn't.

I have lost count of encounters I've had with people who only talk about themselves. They initially ask one question and then steal the conversation and head off on their own agenda until the original topic is lost in a sea of self-appreciation. Attempts to insert oneself into the process are met with incredulity. Why would I want to talk when they are so much more fascinating?

I once sat next to a linoleum layer at dinner on a cruise ship. That evening was painful as there are only so many questions you can ask about floor coverings before you run screaming from the dining room and throw yourself overboard. Funnily enough, he wasn't in the slightest bit interested in anything about me. If he'd given me the chance, I could've made his life so much richer and more interesting. Such a pity!

Words are powerful tools and weapons. Most of us in the Western world enjoy the good fortune of "freedom of speech" but that privilege carries the responsibility of using it with accuracy and compassion. As the old proverb goes—*Death and life are in the power of the tongue.* This from my mum.

5

Artistic Licence

The portrait painter, Sir Malcolm Sergeant, once ruefully stated that, whenever he painted a portrait, he lost a friend. Could it be that, with his artist's eye, he captured a side of his subject that he or she didn't recognise when they looked in the mirror? It's often difficult to see ourselves as others see us.

Then again, great artists are noted for painting what they feel, not always what they see. Those of us without artistic talent are not averse to painting with our tongue, images of friends and family which are not flattering and can be down-right malicious. We throw these words upon a canvas for all to see. They're often touched up and spread at random. Some comments may be as subtle as a fine brush stroke, some are spoken in jest, but all have the power to land indiscriminately and hurt somebody. They can spoil someone's moment or day, or even their life. And the most sobering reality is, we can never paint over them or take them back.

Most people have periods of deep satisfaction in their lives, interspersed with times of disappointment and despair. Either way our casual remarks can throw them. I always had a lot to say and over the years I had to learn that my words also had power.

Farting is such sweet sorrow (with apologies to the Bard).

If you're expecting a flatulence story you've got the wrong end of the stick. I'm pretty sure that all of us have experienced the effects of (as the dictionary said when I consulted it in my 13th year) "an emission from the anus".

Yet every day we pollute the space of others with emissions of another kind—from our mouths; negativity and criticism, foul language, and derogatory statements, just to name a few.

Yes, it may make us feel better. As the old saying goes, "better out than in", but verbal flatulence has no value for anyone but the producer, and life has taught me that selfishness stinks.

As the proverb says...

Pleasant words are like honey, sweet to the soul and healing to the bones.

Shalom

As a word freak, when a friend told me that she'd found some interesting stuff on the internet about the word "shalom", I was onto it. "Shalom" is Jewish for "peace". It's used in Israel as a greeting. But it means a lot more than that. It's a blessing bestowing health, prosperity, welfare—and the absence of discord.

It is, in essence, a prayer for a complete and perfect life. Couldn't we all do with that?

Imagine if we all spoke that kind of blessing into our spouses' and friends' and children's lives. Imagine what could happen if your boss walked up to you every morning and said that he hoped your day would be full of peace, full of harmony and prosperity (maybe with a pay rise to boot).

Imagine if we sent our children to school with the knowledge that when they returned, shalom would reign in their home.

We live in a world that's full of conflict and even if we are far removed from most of it, we all face some kind of battle. We can be thankful for many things; for family, for friends, for comfortable homes, and daily bread. But there are blessings we receive that are beyond our ability and control. These blessings hang on every shalom we speak.

Encouragement

Have you ever noticed how some people make you feel good because their words and manners are positive and up-lifting?

I met someone who said, I'm delighted to meet you. It's a rather old-fashioned word, "delight", but when he said it, I felt good. I headed for my thesaurus and found many synonyms for delight—words like "amuse", "cheer", "thrill" and "satisfy".

This got me thinking about all the people that maybe don't know how much I enjoy them. Or maybe they need a reminder from time to time.

I think communication is becoming very soulless with the advent of email and texting. We tend to exchange information in a language devoid of emotion. We no longer linger over spoken words, savouring the underlying feelings, or celebrating the sheer joy they convey. I've been basking in that word, "delight", for days. There's something about hanging out with people who've passed over to the bright side.

One writer described positive people as "balcony folk". They live on the top of life and encourage everybody to join them as they accentuate the good and downplay the negative. He said,

"... the room lights up when they walk in".

Then there are encounters with people who lambast you with whinges and complaints about almost everybody and everything. The whingers he called "the basement dwellers". They live below life, only popping their heads up to deliver another complaint. They make the room light up when they leave.

What works for me is to invite troubles in for a cup of tea, a cookie, and a good, honest chat, then get them out of the house before they drag me into the basement. Some problems don't even warrant a cookie. They're best left outside the front door.

I see most problems as situations that come to pass, not to move in like a depressing lodger and suck the faith, hope and love out of us.

Wisdom was constantly knocking at my door, teaching me the difference between faith and fantasy. As usual, I learned the hard way. I've never been one for examining my own navel, especially now in my later years when it is increasingly hard to find, but I do like an honest stoush with reality.

I'm no Pollyanna. I know that there are times of trouble and sadness and I must confess I struggle sometimes with ingratitude. There always seems to be someone better off than me and I have to say I relate to the following story.

A man was looking very down in the mouth and his friend asked what was wrong.

"Well", he said, "A few weeks ago my uncle died and left me $40,000."

"And the problem is?" asked his friend.

"It gets worse. Two weeks ago, a cousin died and left me $85,000." He looked even more depressed now. "And just to top it off, last week an aunt died and left me $250,000."

By now his friend was gob smacked. "Why aren't you swinging from the chandeliers? Sounds to me like you're set for life, so what is your problem?"

"Well," he said almost in tears, "This week there's been nothing."

Your and my circumstances may not be this extreme, but I am learning that if I will just listen, I can hear gratitude scratching at my heart.

6

Thanksgiving

I read an eclectic range of literature and always have several books on the go.

At the moment, I'm reading my daughter Tracey's latest novel which she downloaded to my computer, and a biography of Fanny Crosby (a prolific hymn writer).

Another book that challenged me recently was written by a psychiatrist. It was a bit high falutin' for me, but one chapter gave me food for thought. Titled "Gratitude", the author explored some reasons why having a grateful heart increases mental well-being. His experience had shown that grateful people were more likely to recognize life's good gifts than those who thought the world owed them a living. They are also more likely to make others happy and to want to give back to the world. What was particularly interesting was that these people had been subject to all kinds of circumstances, both good and bad.

It seems that good times don't necessarily make people grateful any more than bad times make people bitter. My experience has taught me that a bit of deprivation hones my personal gratitude. We often receive gifts for nothing—a smile, a beautiful sunset, a kind word or even encouragement from a good read. In spiritual terms they're known as "gifts of grace". I'm more convinced than ever that they're ours for the taking and ours for the thanking.

Ups and downs

I went for my daily walk after overcoming my desire for an extra cup of tea. The weather was a bit undecided, so I took my raincoat. I set out to the beach—so far, so good. Then to the shopping centre, and back to the beach. At this stage, I was bathed in sunshine but as I looked out to the horizon, I saw black clouds casting dark shadows over the sea, and that's what I was walking into. It occurred to me that this was a metaphor for life.

I tend towards a positive outlook. I've learned I don't need to look for trouble; sometimes it turns up without invitation.

There can be no smugness about the good times we enjoy, as though we've been singled out for blessing while others have been singled out for trial and tribulation. It's likely that both will visit, often at the same time, and I'm learning to celebrate and endure.

Can we prepare for hard times? Well, my raincoat was a start, but probably no match for lightning, thunder and a howling gale. But we can celebrate with gusto, loving our families and thanking God every day for lessons learned along the way. Hopefully that gratitude will help us to imbibe a glass half-full.

Toughen Up

I read a column by Deborah Hill Cone titled, "Suffering, It's So Good for You".

In it she says, "It's the pain theory. You know those people who have tidy lives, who don't wake up in the night with un-named dread, don't feel mad and otherworldly as hell…I just used to think they didn't have the right to have their opinions about anything taken seriously because they hadn't suffered enough to be listened to".

The article struck a chord with me because, during my poor days, I often endured conversations with reasonably well-off people about the challenges of finding just the right furniture, or caterer, or holiday to pop their corks. I comforted a sobbing acquaintance as she shared her husband's trauma when their boat had to be sold due to a business downturn. Secretly I was trying not to slap her in the face.

The complexities of life do hit you right between the eye-balls and I was reminded of this as I sat watching the news. There was a piece on Victoria Beckham launching herself into American society. She was photographed pitching the first ball at a baseball game, in *ultra* short-shorts and designer haircut. Oops, do I hear a miaow?

Then they interviewed her about getting settled in LA. It was a Big Problem evidently, as she struggled to, "…find a house and schools and a good manicurist". I hope she nailed it.

Meanwhile, back on planet solo mother, I woke up each night trying to work out how to make three meals out of lefto-vers. In fact, I think I ate leftovers for years, never remembering what the original meal was.

Suffering for most of us is a certainty, like death and taxes. Some people endure horrendous pain and loss and the chal-lenge is always how to turn that pain into something of value.

Where the suffering may not be that extreme, we can choose to embrace faith in a better future and to practice gratitude for all the good things.

Back on the farm

We were tethered to the weather. Our very livelihood depended on spring and summer rains. I appreciate in hindsight this grassroots grounding. I considered my education at a two-roomed country school to be top-notch, but it wasn't that hard to be top of the class when there were only six students. I suspect this is where I developed an inflated sense of my success. High school was a reality check. My world was getting bigger.

Me and country life were not a good fit. I tried so hard to embrace it but always had my nose pressed against the window pane of a bigger world.

However, living close to the land does give you a make-do attitude. What my father could fix with a piece of No. 8 wire was limitless—from cars, to machinery to household goods. I learned how to milk the cows and feed the pigs. These may not sound like major skills, but they played into my belief that anything is possible.

I even raised a pet lamb, although Lambikins disappeared one day. Dad said he'd swapped him for one from the neighbour, as we sat down to a dinner of delicious lamb chops.

We ate well from a burgeoning organic vegetable garden and a small fridge often stuffed to the brim with a whole sheep.

Runt piglets were kept alive in the hot water cupboard and hand-fed to protect them from their dreadful mothers, hell-bent on stomping them to death. The irony of raising them this way so we could eat them later has not eluded me!

Farming methods have evolved over the years with some farmers coming to terms with farming practice being a possible pollutant of our pristine environment. I've been following with huge interest the government's idea of a flatulence tax. I, of course, say this tongue in cheek. The idea of thousands of bureaucrats running around counting sheep or cows' emissions is too hilarious for words.

But let's say it does happen that every month, undercover flatulence officers speed down country roads, pop in for tea and scones with the local farmers, get out their highly technical gasometers and do their task. Will they measure purely by stock numbers, or could there be a gadget that measures output? Maybe there's special fodder for cattle, to reduce the amount of polluting gas that cattle produce, and they could then receive a rebate for good behaviour. Surely there's an opportunity here for a budding entrepreneur to invent a process to harness all that energy. Maybe each cowshed could have a special gas tank installed. As the cows chew their cud and let down their milk, a hose from their derrieres could deliver this priceless energy to the storage tank. This energy could, in turn, power the milking machines—or the farmer's TV, for that matter. Or it could be piped to Parliament for internal consumption—although I suspect they already have enough hot air down there.

Whatever happens, this bizarre situation is supplying us all with a few laughs and for that I thank them all from the heart of my bottom.

Sex education was in-your-face. I remember peeking around the corner of the cowshed one day to see the vet artificially inseminating a cow. His hand disappeared up to his armpit. I almost threw up.

When I was about to give birth to my first child, I asked Mum if she had been embarrassed at the presence of all the medical staff watching and helping with the process. She said that by that stage you'd be happy for an orangutan to deliver your baby. No primates were present at any of my births, but I kept it in mind in case one turned up. This rather wacky sense of humour was the hallmark of our family and has served me well in many of life's challenges.

There was an unfortunate incident with a hapless chicken. Dad had wrung its neck and planned to pluck it later; but it didn't die and we found it running around with its head at a funny angle. We may have gone vegetarian for dinner that night.

A family concert many years later caused a rewrite of a famous song to the *Bantam of the Opera*. For many years, we didn't just have get-togethers; we had major production numbers pooling our various talents. We, of course, basked in the light of Mum's relentless adoration of us. Some of our concerts were legendary. I remember one item performed by Michael Flatulence called *Lord of The Prance*, set in an Irish bog with suitable sound effects. Tobesure, tobesure.

Dad played the trumpet in the RNZAF band, and we spent many nights around the piano aptly played by Robin or Richard, singing our hearts out. Tears still well over every time I hear Mario Lanza singing *Oh My Papa.* I played the spoons, although it was pretty obvious that this talent would not get me a starring role on stage.

8

City Lights

E. B White, of *Charlotte's Web* fame, said, "In every man's life, there comes a time when you have to be fully awake instead of half asleep." For me, when the time came, it meant moving to the city where I negotiated the complexities of a real, well-paid, government job. My being bubbled with possibilities. A city of over a million must surely have been waiting for my arrival...or not.

At about this time, I found Jesus, and in some ways that made things worse. If I hopped on God's bandwagon then nothing was impossible. It took me a while to realise that I was not God's gift to God!

My faith journey was accompanied by attempts to make belief and reality my friends.

Anne Lamott wrote:

"I do not at all understand the mystery of grace—only that it meets us where we are but does not leave us where it found us. Hope begins in the dark, the stubborn hope that if you just show up and try to do the right thing, the dawn will come. You wait and watch and work: You don't give up. Certainty is missing the point entirely. Faith includes noticing the mess, the emptiness and discomfort, and letting it be there until some light returns."

I found faith is messy and unpredictable and full of mystery. Yet through all my stuff-ups, all my lettings-down-of-the-side, I know I'm saturated with love and grace that won't come from you or you or you. And I don't blame you one little bit. Sometimes I can't stand me either.

A wise person once said, if you find the perfect church don't join it... you'll ruin it. If you're a believer, pray for a sense of humour. Pursed lips and furrowed brows are so not fun.

And if God is watching us, the least we can do is be entertaining.

Bruce Almighty

I watched a corny movie, *Bruce Almighty*, starring Jim Carrey with Morgan Freeman as God. Poor old Bruce had been having a rough time and gave God an earful about his lot in life. God finally decided he'd had enough of Bruce's complaints so he handed over his job.

There were two rules: Bruce wasn't allowed to tell anyone that he was God and he wasn't allowed to interfere with people's free will.

At first, it's great fun. Bruce conjures up a fabulous car for himself, gets the job he always wanted and generally creates mayhem in the world. Unfortunately, in the process, he loses the love and respect of his girlfriend and must sort out what is really important.

At one stage the real God gives him a few pointers. He says, "If you want to see a miracle you have to be a miracle."

I'd heard it described another way. "We need to be part of the answer to every prayer we pray."

It makes me think twice about the things I ask for. Am I prepared to step in and help people, to be part of a miracle for them? I know the trouble in the world—or even in my own neighbourhood—can seem overwhelming. But someone has to say "enough's enough" and be involved in the solution. Maybe if we all felt like this, we could indeed be the hands and feet of God.

Anne Lamott says,

"Again and again, I tell God I need help, and God says, 'Well, isn't that fabulous? Because I need help too. So, you go get that old woman over there some water, and I'll figure out what we're going to do about your stuff.'"

It took me a while to realise that I didn't want God's job despite my long chats with Him about his management style.

9

Acts of God

World weather patterns have been weird lately. It seems like all hell's been let loose. I'm sure insurance companies all over the world are poring over claims and figuring out if these events are "Acts of God" or "Global Warming" or mere coincidences.

All the suffering makes me wonder if God is a real meanie. I wonder if He sits in heaven wringing his hands and scheming who He should zap next. Should He flood the Muslims because they've been mean to the Christians? But then he'd have to deal with the Christians 'cos they've been mean to the Muslims at times. Then he'd have to figure out whether the Jews ("God's chosen people" for crying out loud) should be buried in molten ash or turned to salt for giving up the Gaza Strip. And how about them Palestinians with their suicide bombers? Shouldn't they get a plague or two for their sins?

As I write this, I remember times when it seemed that my world was being flooded or blown to bits without hope of ever recovering. And I remember acts that were so good—money out of the blue, and people who showed great kindness when I couldn't cry any more. I recall invisible peace, strange encouraging circumstances I could have never orchestrated.

I suspect that they were the real, useful acts of God.

Faith, Hope, Love

How many times in the night, God,
Have we shared heart's deepest needs?
How many times have I wondered
If faith is present at all?

You have searched me, and I know
That your love seeks truth, for real;
Not self-absorbed, starry, faith centre-stage,
But a sorry heart, broken and soft.

My search is often questionable,
Fraught with selfishness and stumbling.
I can't take credit for faith
Placed sovereignly, graciously.

My only part is a panic-stricken heart
Crying "God help me!"
And I guess that's why you're God and
I'm not and that's OK with me.

Despite my obvious gifts, I couldn't boss God around. For reasons beyond me He had no plans to be my heavenly magician, conjured up at will to do my bidding. He is otherly, and all through my life I've had to learn to stand aside and let His will be done.

Nevertheless, it is so cool to be able to talk to Him all day and night, to offload the stresses of the day and know that someone is listening. And yet, I find the subject of prayer rather mysterious. I mean, we talk to God and tell him everything that's going on in our lives even though He knows it all already.

Because I had nothing to lose, I thought I'd try just talking to God like He was in the room or at least outside my front door. So, I started with a short morning plea asking that I'd be reasonably successful that day. I asked that I'd be kind and aware of other people's struggles and that I might be helpful. Then one day I read a prayer at a funeral to bring some comfort to all of us who'd had to say goodbye to a dear friend.

During any one day, I said I was sorry for my insensitivity and selfishness. This prayer seemed to flow rather too often for my liking! I asked for my friends and family to know that someone cared. I prayed for our hurting world, I prayed against injustice and bigotry and hatred.

And finally, I prayed thanks; thanks for this beautiful world, for my children and grandchildren, for the freesias blooming in gratitude for some spring sunshine. My meagre attempts at prayer have triggered something rather special. It was well put by these words, "Prayer is the breathing of the heart".

Newsflash! It's a Fact...

God is bigger and better than you.

A friend who's a drug and alcohol counsellor shared this with me.

Some of her clients are resistant to that part of the Twelve Step program where they admit they can't deliver themselves from their addiction and must place themselves in the hands of a "higher power". They see that kind of submission as a crutch, something for wimps. They'll wriggle and writhe, protesting that they're able to fix the problem themselves.

My friend wisely suggests that the reason why they feel no need for a higher power is because they already serve one and it's drugs and/or alcohol and/or gambling. They're friendly "gods" at first, readily available, and creating a great feeling of well-being. But over time they demand a heavy penalty, the complete sacrifice of your whole life, and the right to control and destroy. We are free to choose addiction but eventually it chooses us, and its power is more than we could ever imagine. A "no-brainer" really.

10

My desire to save the world was not quite going as I hoped. Even my attempts at passing on my faith legacy sometimes came to nothing.

Babes' Mouths

My oldest granddaughter, Amelia, was quite distraught when her mum and dad said they were leaving for the Middle East. I tried to be brave, but I have to say it was heart-wrenching when they left. My other grandchildren had lived overseas for years. I'd enjoyed being a hands-on grandma to Amelia in her early years, and her mum and I are great friends.

To help her settle into her new country, I gave Amelia a stuffed alpaca that I'd bought in Peru; and I taught her to pray, holding the alpaca, and asking God to be her special friend.

I've never pressured the kids about my faith, but I think that children need someone to talk to when nobody else seems to understand. We parents are so flawed, and we don't have all the answers to their needs. We may even be part of their problems at times and I think it's good for them to know that there's a ready ear when life tumbles down.

Prayer can give them strength and hope and faith and peace and to deprive them of the knowledge of such resources would be a real pity.

A few months later, while talking to my daughter on Skype, she said Amelia had been having a hard time adjusting. I asked how the alpaca cuddling was going on. There was an awkward pause, then my daughter said. "Oh, Mum, I'm so sorry, but the dog ate the alpaca!"

So much for my contribution to her spiritual heritage.

This same wee girl had a lesson for mankind on a beautiful starry night in Auckland…

Babes and Sucklings

I took four-year-old Amelia to see the Christmas lights in a city street. She skipped up and down, mesmerised. Here was Santa waving from an attic, and reindeer and elves and angels twinkling up the walls, in the gardens, and over the roofs.

"Fantastico", she shouted, her blue eyes open as wide as they could get. She made a little friend and together they ran and gasped and celebrated as only children can do. At the top of the street we took a break, and she had hot chocolate with a marshmallow on top. I thought she would pop from all the excitement.

By now it was nine p.m. and she was a little sleepy, so the walk back was slower. Then suddenly she stopped and looked very worried.

"What's the matter?" I asked.

"Well," she said, "I think baby Jesus would be very sad right now."

"Why?" I asked.

"Because all the people love the lights more than Him." Then she trotted to the car.

It took me a minute to compose myself. One sentence from the mouth of a babe had summed up the whole meaning of Christmas.

Rather than trying to save the world, it occurred to me that faith is best worked out in our own families and communities.

God continually asks me, "What do you have in your hands?" As I look down at them, I know I can help, care, and love without flash or fanfare and that's OK with me.

Pick'n'mix

A friend and I were coffeeing, having an almost friendly discussion about the pros and cons of faith.

"I don't believe in any of that rubbish" she said, "although I do believe, as a society, we should live by a set of agreed rules like the Ten Commandments."

I said, *"Well the first one is You shall have no other gods before Me."*

"Oh no, not that one!" was her response.

And herein lies the weakness of a pick'n'mix values system where every man sees freedom as license to do whatever he wants. I guess you can't legislate faith.

There are seven things the Lord cannot stand: a proud look, a lying tongue, hands that kill innocent people, a mind that thinks up evil plans, feet that are quick to do evil, a witness who lies, and someone who starts arguments among families. *Proverbs 6:16-19*

These look like pretty good words to live by.

Years ago, Coca Cola ran a campaign with the slogan, *"It's the real thing, what the world needs today."* At the same time there were letters to the editor rubbishing Christianity as a religion for "crutch-needers" who couldn't do life on their own. I couldn't resist writing to the paper with this little rejoinder.

The Real Thing

So, God doesn't exist? I wish I'd known that because for many years I've endeavoured to follow Him in vain. I've endured all that wasted peace in the midst of many trials.

I've shared incredible conversations with my imaginary friend and been inspired by His fictitious words. My life has been filled with fake comfort and out-of-this-world wisdom. I've known phony protection, false security and fabricated joy.

And just to top it off. I'm still believing I will spend eternity in the presence of my precious Hoax. And to think, I could've had a Coke. After all, "…it's the real thing, what the world needs today".

11

Let's Back up a Bit

While figuring out how to make my new-found faith work, I went to University and studied Spanish. Maybe God had an Iberian mission for me. My heart leapt as I wandered the halls of academia. It was here I realised I lacked the application to get a degree. I was rudderless, and also lonely in the big city, and found it difficult to work full-time and study at night. It was a shock, coming from a home where I was served three square meals a day to fending for myself with other flat mates who stole my food. This was the 1960s when women became nurses, teachers, or secretaries—or got married.

And then I met a lovely man. In hindsight, I needed a cross between Prince Charming and Bill Gates; one was a fantasy and the other hadn't been born yet. I married at twenty, and four children came quickly because that was what you did. I loved being a mum and thought I could shake off this drive for fulfilment, or I could find fulfilment in my husband and children. I thought I could grow up to *not be me.*

After losing everything in a few business deals, we decided to move to California to try our luck there.

In hindsight, my husband did not think this through very

well because I now found myself in a place where women ruled! Most American women had careers and they had a lot to say about everything. I did a course in community involvement, volunteered at our children's schools, and loved the climate.

I threw myself into California life, although I found many people I met were shallow and materialistic. At a sales dinner one night, I met a particularly lip-pumped dolly-bird who was very excited when she saw a small octopus in the restaurant aquarium. "Look at all his testicles," she gasped. Look indeed!

A saleswoman asked me where I was from and when I told her, she asked how long it had taken us to drive to California. Another person told me I spoke just like the Queen. I'm sure Her Majesty would've rolled over in her tiara at that one.

They say that a big shot is a little shot away from home and I was viewed with awe as I turned up to dinners with pavlovas. A friend had brought me some passionfruit pulp from New Zealand, so I told the guests it was an aphrodisiac. Wow! was I popular after that!

My saving grace was my best friend Shirley, who hailed from Tulsa, Oklahoma. She got the Kiwi sense of humour and together we had many adventures. One day we were offered an entire orchard of apples to pick from. We drove out of town a couple of hours, found the orchard, filled the boot of the car with apples, and brought them to a local charity which fed homeless people.

It was with her that Papa Smith's Lollipops was established. For months we padded around on sticky floors, churning out sugared treats and selling them in local shops.

By now I had a new child and the huge responsibility of providing for four children weighed heavily. I found it difficult to be the poor family around town. One Christmas we were given so many frozen turkeys that I had to store them in the bath. It was a good lesson in giving—that you give according to the need instead of off-loading unwanted poultry. Bear in mind that a twenty-pound turkey could be bought for $6.99. Most of them ended up in the garbage.

One lady asked me how I managed to feed so many children given our on-going problems. My Kiwi hackles rose, and I told her I fed them alternate days to keep the grocery bills down. I think she believed me.

The financial problems that had dogged us in New Zealand continued and after we lost our house, I lost my will to make it work. There were other problems in the marriage, but this is my story and I don't think it's fair to labour the points.

After much angst I left, taking my four bewildered children with me, setting off on a journey that in hindsight could've gone horribly wrong. There was always a possibility that we would return to the USA but deep down I knew that was not going to happen.

* * *

We boarded a plane back to New Zealand and I now found myself…

12

Sleeping Single in a Double Bed

The sense of freedom was exhilarating. I could turn my visions into reality and take the rap if I fell in my face. Emotionally, I was spent, and determined to never fall in love again. I decided I was better off without attaching any romantic feelings to anyone or anything. I would be a machine, devoted to the children's future, and building a new life for us all.

Nevertheless, I could not be cavalier about what we faced as a family. The children missed their dad and the life they had in America. There were no Dunkin Donuts, no Denny's, no multiple TV channels, and no outlet malls. They had to wear school uniforms.

Even though I knew I had to leave, the enormity of my decision haunted me. I had broken my marriage vows "for better for worse, until death us do part". And the children were distraught.

I probably decided I wanted to leave my marriage a long time before I actually walked out. But I was in for some unexpected shocks when I finally flew home to New Zealand.

My husband's grandmother called and gave me a real telling-off. "How could I abandon her grandson and how dare I break my marriage vows?"

My children suffered, emotionally and socially, as they adapted to an almost foreign culture. It took a long time for the family to recover and for me to re-establish old social ties and make new friends.

When you stop being married, you're still the same person. So, you naturally expect others to treat you the same as always. I think that happens in the case of a death; people may not understand what you're going through, but they still regard you more-or-less as they did before.

Death is accepted, but a marriage break-up—that's different. That's a mistake! People think it's something that should've been avoided, something that should've been fixed. The trouble was that most people never knew of the problems in our marriage. I guess they saw us as a happy couple.

Some old friends became very candid about the state of their own marriages and occasionally I was perceived as a threat. It brought out a lot of insecurities in the people around me. One friend involved in a marriage break-up when she was young, now began laying all her bad feelings on me—feelings she'd never let out at the time.

The shock for many of my friends and family was huge. There's nothing like living in a foreign country to hide your failure and my innate optimism had let me down. I am now very cynical when people think moving far away will fix their problems.

I returned with $4000. By the time we rented a house, paid school fees and purchased uniforms, I had $800 left and so I got stuck in. I resurrected my Californian lollipop manufacturing business and that lifted us above the breadline until my youngest was older and I could get a "real" job.

I even got into a legal battle with a large confectionery company who didn't like the name of my kiwi-shaped lollipop. After a bit of back and forth I sold them the name and moved on to other things.

I completed a diploma in travel as another string to my bow. In my spare time I ran around the city selling lunches out of baskets. My official title was "Bun Runner" although I felt more like a basket case. I chucked that in when a customer said she caught semolina from one of my chicken sandwiches!

The children were amazing. They were often roped into my schemes. We stuffed envelopes and delivered papers. We salvaged furniture off the side of the road, and I learnt at what time of day meat at the supermarket dropped to half price. If we needed extra money, I cleaned houses, did gardening, and even catered a wedding. Our food was basic, nutritious but not fancy.

Richard is now a gourmet cook, spurred on by the fear that he would have to eat like we did then for the rest of his life.

I rented a house in a good school district and took on two boarders to help pay the rent. After being shoved around from one house to another, I decided we needed to buy a house. I shared my dilemma with a friend, and she offered to lend me $5,000 and give me another $5,000; we went house-hunting.

I found a small townhouse with two bedrooms upstairs and a garage underneath. A builder friend converted the garage into two extra bedrooms and we now had a home of our own. Emily and I slept in the lounge until the building work finished. The laundry was in one of the bedrooms and Richard laughs as he remembers trying to sleep to the swish of the washing machine.

One night, while he was out, the washing machine became unbalanced while spinning and leapt across his room, spraying suds like snowflakes all over the room.

Five of us in a tiny house was do-able until we were all infected by a tummy bug at the same time, both ends. One bathroom was underwhelming or, should I say, overflowing!

We learned a lot together

I guess, like many of you, life for me has been a tough journey at times. Some of my trips were planned. Some I was dragged into with determined resistance, and some left me wondering, "If life is a two-way street, how come I get run over in both directions? I formed life axioms that informed my path.

- That it's not worth getting your knickers in a twist, it ruins the knickers and makes you walk funny.
- That we would be less concerned about what people thought of us if we realized how little they thought of us.
- Pain is inevitable, misery is optional, so stick a geranium in your hat and be happy.
- If you can't see the light at the end of the tunnel, march up there and light the darn thing yourself.

My mantra was being forged.

"You don't know that you can't..." became a constant reminder. Doubts and fears were bludgeoned into submission as I hacked my way through life. As long as I kept my longings in check, we were good to go.

As the single mum of four children, I somehow managed to feed them, educate them, and keep the odd bit of clothing on their backs. I'm sure if you asked them, they'd say it wasn't ideal and that deep, valuable friendships were threatened by their lack of designer clothes and limitless spending money. My children said that they learned early the connection between work and money. They learned that pride is often only skin deep, but dignity and humility go right to the heart.

They learned the joy of accomplishment through perseverance. They learned that you really could survive when your peers don't like you, don't include you, or don't make you one of the "in" crowd. Designer clothes and shoes do not "maketh the man".

I strongly believe it's the parent's job to make sure the children rise above their parenting and, in my case, that has happened.

Just for the record, I'm expecting to be well-cared for in my old age, although will not hold my breath on that one.

13

Peer Pressure

Wisdom knocked at my door and told me not to worry about what others thought unless I had to live with them.

Outside your close family and friends, most people won't give you a second thought. Not everybody will like you. Sometimes you are horrible.

Ask for forgiveness for being mean, late or rude; but not for being yourself.

And so, I forged on despite constant financial pressure and times of feeling alone.

But there was nearly always one more squirt of toothpaste and one more square of toilet paper. Occasionally I bought one roll at a time to tide us over until payday. Flush we weren't, but caught short, never; and there was always some newspaper hanging around.

If we ran out of anything I just went out and found a way to make a few bucks. I stopped short of being a lady-of-the-night as I liked my sleep too much and, despite my positivity, was probably afraid nobody would pick me up and I'd have to pay someone to take me away! Also, I'm a morning person so may have fallen asleep on the job.

The teenage years were a real challenge. I became like a random breath-testing policeman, stalking them, contacting other parents and staying up until they were all home.

One night I had a call from a youth aid officer to say that my child had been smoking pot in a park after she sneaked out of a police-sponsored disco. The irony of this does not escape me. We conspired to deal with this:

That night I answered the phone and passed it to her. The officer evidently told her that, if she got a marijuana conviction on her passport, she wouldn't ever be able to return to the USA. Her face blanched as I watched from the kitchen.

"Who was that?" I asked when she hung up.

"Just a friend checking something out," she said as she fled to her room. (When she was twenty-one, I told her what I'd done.)

Another time, I heard her creeping up the driveway and getting in a car, so I jumped in my car and followed them all the way to the beach and turned my lights on full while she tried to slide down in the back seat. The callow youth obviously decided this mother was too much trouble and took her home. That was fun!

I know they got up to other hijinks and I was worried sick most of the time but could only deal with the things I knew about.

I stumbled on this tactic as my girls began dating.

One slightly rough-around-the-edges young man turned up one night to pick up Emily for a date. The car he drove had obviously been modified as it rumbled into the driveway. I could tell it was his pride and joy. I asked him how he would feel if I took it for a spin and came back with a dent in the driver's door. He was horrified to say the least.

I said, "My precious daughter is more valuable than a top line BMW and I expect her to be returned in the same condition as she left." (Emily hid behind the door by this stage.)

It worked and I can't remember his name or the make of car he drove.

Burden on the Taxpayer

Although I was statistically a mother with potentially at-risk children, it never occurred to me that we were disadvantaged. I encouraged the children to do everything with all their heart, soul and mind, even if they didn't succeed. There would always be critics, but a willing heart is unstoppable.

I knew they'd never be perfect. With me being their mother, what chance did they have of that? I learned that the most wonderful thing about parenting is that your children turn out, to some extent, to be like you. It's also the most terrifying. As their parent, I know that building a sense of values does not happen automatically. They are usually acquired because it's more painful to disregard them. I discovered, for instance that pinching one's sister was very successfully stopped by me pinching the offender's pocket money.

I've also observed that most children, left to their own devices, will lean more towards dodgy values than good ones.

A child therapist told me that a useful tool in discipline was what she called "the goods and services tax". A parent provides "the goods" as long as the child behaves appropriately. No arguments are necessary as a desperately wanted lift to the mall or the movies is only forthcoming if the bed is made and the chores are done. No tax? No goods and services.

Give them Wings

There's a down-side to this relentless possibility-grasping.

It means your children will, to some extent, be fearless as well. In hindsight I should've tried to make them afraid of flying because they all left me and went to live on the other side of the world. They flew to Canada and America and Sydney and Qatar.

I'd hardly heard of Qatar when my son-in-law announced he had a pilot's job in Doha and would be kidnapping my daughter and two gorgeous granddaughters to live there for a few years. I didn't care that the wages were good, and they'd be able to set themselves up financially. Who in their right mind would want to live in the desert where temperatures soar to the 50°Cs?

I tried to terrify the daylights out of them, but they just looked at me as though I was mad. I asked God if it was necessary for me to populate most of the continents in the world. He didn't answer and deep down I knew it was pointless to rave on. Kiwis generally do very well overseas. It's something to do with being a hop, step and a jump from our pioneering roots. We're considered adaptable and willing to try, and it's reflected in our global presence in many fields. So far, my children contribute in writing, human resources, e-commerce, and early childhood education. I guess I'll have to leave the fields of rocket science and brain surgery to their offspring.

14

Pee Party

Many factors determine whether you'll be successful in life. Where you're born, what sort of education you have, if your parents were positive or negative about your abilities, to name a few. But our belief system is probably the biggest asset or handicap we have. Someone once said, "Those who think they can and those who think they can't are probably both right."

Some belief systems give us a false definition of success. We may have come to believe that money, fame, and the way we look are the most important arbiters of life's success.

Shallow values are fed by the media in magazines and on TV as we see pencil-thin models wobbling along catwalks supposedly portraying ideal women. Male models don't just have six-pack abs, some have ten or twelve-packs, and I suspect extras are bought online.

We're told we need to use a certain make of makeup because "We're worth it"; or to wear certain clothes that tell the world, "I've got the look". But the one that takes the cake for me is the ad telling me, "Don't let a weak bladder hold you back". At seventy, I'm reminded that I could be missing the mark. I've decided to dismiss this advice. To me it's just a storm in a pee-cup.

Like you, I'm surrounded with doom and gloom. Many jobs are at risk, the world economy is at tipping point and violence continues to erupt everywhere, including in God's Own.

I mused about this as I drove over the Auckland Harbour Bridge the other day.

It was windy and the New Zealand flags flew flat out, buffeted, straining from the flagpole, trying desperately not to shred and float away in the harbour.

Somehow, I found them inspiring.

When there's no wind they hang lifeless and the full extent of their glory can't be seen.

History shows us that civilizations are unable to sustain endless times of plenty. Flourishing societies become self-indulgent and flabby; excesses ruin their health and remove incentives to work hard. Authorities abuse their power, then rebellion and anarchy follow. Nobody wants tough times, but they can be a "wake-up call" inducing us to examine what's really important.

After a few hard knocks, I took a good look at myself and acknowledged I was hopelessly flawed. I longed for authenticity, to feel the sense that my inner motivation and outward behavior had synergy. But to be authentic, you need unconditional love from someone.

Sometimes I forget how much God loves me. More than that, He knows me and still loves me.

This was reinforced many years ago when my youngest daughter was very ill in Auckland Children's hospital. Along a corridor someone had painted a mural of the Velveteen Rabbit story. I remembered reading this story to the kids and this specific quote came to mind. "'Real isn't how you're made,' said the Skin Horse. 'It's a thing that happens to you. When a child loves you for a long, long time, not just to play with, but REALLY loves you, then you become real.'"

I temporarily lost sight of this love-being-enough later in life, but at this time I was good to go. Emily recovered and life went on.

15

Pure of heart?

I'm always suspicious of my own motives. I'm an extrovert and must remind myself that my relentless need to connect with people is because I crave an audience, not because I'm riddled with compassion.

I feel uncomfortable when someone tells me I'm a good person. I'd never hold myself up as a "pillar of the community". "Pillory of the community" sits better. I know me, I live with me, and there's no answer for holier-than-thou. I've observed that principles combined with self-righteousness are not a pretty sight. I'm analytical about the problems people voice and suspicious of people who gossip "because they care". Yeah, right.

I remember a story about a group of Christians confessing their shortcomings to each other. Evidently, some juicy stories were told, and everyone nodded "with compassion". That is, until it was Mildred's turn. She said she'd struggled all her life with gossip. The meeting ended abruptly.

On the subject of sins, I suspect that comparing ourselves to others is way up there. I've found my measuring myself against others is inaccurate. I either feel superior or inferior. So, I've abandoned that process in favour of getting on with what I do best and trying to maintain a modicum of modesty.

I'm a firm believer in original sin. My observation is that people—even young children—will attempt to get their own way given the choice.

Do we get what we deserve? That's a moot point—both good and bad. Do bad things happen to good people? They do, all the time, and I haven't a clue why. Do ratbags get their comeuppance? Occasionally, but not nearly enough for my liking. Once again, I'm reminded that nobody has set me up to be the world's judge and jury.

I strongly believe that life owes me nothing. I relentlessly resisted developing a victim mentality. I celebrated the risks and looked for opportunities. As I scooted along my solo journey on the bones of my backside, I learned the joy of sharing my resources. When I had extra, I gave it away, fearless about running out.

I've observed two ways a person can go if they're deprived. They're either deeply grateful when things improve, or they assume a sense of entitlement to everything and become a bottomless pit of "more, more, more".

Gratitude for everything became my life's breath. I praised God for my hot shower, finding mushrooms on special in the supermarket, and having a car full of fuel.

I learned the hard way to negotiate for just about everything I bought. Financial constraints meant I couldn't afford driving lessons for the children, so I taught them to drive. I was not good at this. I was convinced they were trying to kill me as they swerved, narrowly missing every other vehicle on the street.

Another of my failings was DIY. Anyone observing me painting a wall would be tempted to yell, "Frances, step away from the brush...."

Circumstances conspired to force me to attempt projects year after year. Practice didn't make perfect and I lurched from one mediocre result to the next, hoping no-one noticed my blunders. If the saying "God loves a trier" is true, He must be exceptionally fond of me. In fact, I've pondered the possibility that I should be charged with a felony for the incompetence I've inflicted on poor unsuspecting projects.

DIY to me is like being DIC of tools. I've toyed with the idea of having a couple of glasses of pinot beforehand to make the process less painful—and perhaps more fun—but I sensed that alcohol would not enhance my performance.

I'm heartened that there are things that I'm really good at. I've produced four strapping, healthy children, and led hundreds of unsuspecting travelers around the world without losing a single tour member. I've managed to enjoy a fascinating career in writing, travel, confectionery manufacturing, and bun-running, to name a few.

None of my children have turned out to be Texas axe murderers, they're all potty-trained and have busily produced nine grandchildren with excellent genetics.

I guess I can't be exceptional at everything. As for the DIY, I may just have to be kinder to myself and understand that I too am a work in progress. In the face of this philosophizing...

Occasionally life just sucks

As a nervous flyer was contemplating a trip, her philosophical friend commented that one must be prepared for all possibilities. "After all," she mused, "if it's your time to go, it's your time to go."

The traveler thought for a moment and asked, "But what if it's the pilot's time to go?"

I've read dozens of books and heard dozens of doyens rattle on about the Power of Positive Thinking. You may have heard the saying that all problems are just opportunities in disguise.

I ask, "If I jump out of a plane and my parachute fails, do I have a problem or an opportunity?"

Wisdom tells me to stay on terra firma, but if I must jump, make sure my life insurance payments are up-to-date.

There are times when you must dig in, hold on, or just scream at the injustice of life.

When a friend offered to teach my son to drive, I was so grateful.

Wisdom is about low expectations of things I can't control. I had a growing sense of responsibility for my happiness.

16

New Year's Resolutions

Have you noticed that, when you're unhappy, even those close to you have a short attention span? I found, to my chagrin, that misery loves company and it isn't mine. I wanted to feel more contented and was thinking about how to make this a reality.

I can't look back because the past has gone, and many memories are distorted by time. The "good old days" probably weren't that good and the "bad old days…". Well, I survived them.

I can't continue to blame others for my state. Forgiveness has to figure high on the agenda.

Being grateful for what I have is a sure way to be happy. Hankering after my neighbour's car, his boat, his ox, or her spouse, is a quick road to misery.

I let go of what I'd never have: for me, a figure like Elle McPherson, a house like the Sultan of Brunei's. Dream a little, be happy in your own company and reach out to others in need.

Laugh a lot, especially at yourself. I think I'm a bumbling, stumbling mass of hilarity, and don't get me started on you. It's working for me already. Endorphins are kicking in and I pick this year to be a real winner.

Single Parenting is "Not for the Faint-Hearted"

Did this mean there weren't nights when I cried into my large tumbler of cheap wine? You betcha.

But once again another axiom would ring in my ear... "Get off the cross, we need the wood." Then I'd look at my tear-stained face in the bathroom mirror and get the giggles. I guess nowadays I would take a selfie and post it on Facebook and get hundreds of "Likes"—or not.

I'm a sharer. Mostly, I'm relaxed about not having time or resources to myself. But one thing I coveted as a single mum was to be able to wallow in my own disease without someone else stealing my medical thunder.

When the children were little, the usual spate of childhood illnesses made their spotty, snotty, pooey way into our household. Now, nursing is not my forte. I am uninterested in the mechanics of disease. While doctors explain a "procedure" to me, I ask them politely to just treat me and not bore me with the details. My children affectionately (I think) call me "Florence Nightmare".

Sometimes you can't even share your latest ailment with friends because it turns out they have something worse; theirs is obviously more riveting to them than is mine.

Back to me and my terrible dose of the very impressive, bronchio-spastic bronchitis I caught in the middle of a California summer.

"Here's my chance," I thought. "I can be cossetted and cuddled and fed chicken soup. I'll milk this for all it's worth."

Within a week the whole family was sick. Croup, chest infections, even pneumonia. And guess who became chief nurse and bottlewasher? Yours truly—bedecked in a surgical mask, breathlessly chasing a two-year old boy from pillar to post. I was literally Florence Nightmare on steroids thanks to a doctor who extorted $175 for the privilege. Sadly, my saga ended with my malady unrecorded in the annals of history. I suspect other participants in the drama don't even remember the name of the disease I had.

And the horrid truth is, the virus may have started with me!

17

**A joyful heart is good medicine, but a crushed
spirit dries up the bones.**
Proverbs 17:22

Some people comment that I never let life get me down even
when I've worked so hard to get anywhere.

I can't take any credit for the nature that I've been given. I've
always had a cheerful disposition. When heading down the
path of negativity I haven't found it much fun, so have turned
around and headed back to where I belong.

Developing character and virtue is a different kettle of fish.
I'm convinced that lurking inside me is a percentage of narcis-
sism. I want an easy life; I want it done my way; and I certainly
don't want to suffer the consequences of my actions. I suspect
it's all your fault, not mine.

To my surprise I've found you don't learn virtues by being
unvirtuous. My prayer, "God give me patience and give it right
now" has not been consistently successful. All the challenging
virtues—compassion, perseverance, longsuffering, and tolerance, to name a few—are not learned by floating on fluffy

clouds or soaking in champagne in a tub. They are forged in the crucibles of life's relentless lessons. We have a choice about taking them on board. I know I'm a hypocrite, and if you're my friend, you may have noticed also. Given your failings as well as mine, we could be soulmates!

At one difficult stage on my journey I was greatly inspired by New Zealand's bid to win the Americas Cup. I could understand the challenge of tipping your hat at something almost impossible—a Don Quixotic mission.

I wrote to Michael Fay and our team and said the following…

We can be a funny bunch, we Kiwis. When someone achieves the impossible, we envy him. If he doesn't try, we accuse him of laziness or cowardice. No wonder we've been called "a passionless people". We neutralise each other into the safety of mass mediocrity.

That is, until there's a chance we could pull off a coup, until we can prove the big guy doesn't always have to win, until an Aussie or a Yank reminds us of our size and tries to put us in our place. Our hackles rise, the national adrenalin flows and it's "anchors aweigh".

Now the Americas Cup is upon us again. I'm encouraged by Michael Fay's initiative and perseverance and it's inspired me to believe great things for myself and my crew at home. My four children and I must refit our boat and sail through rough and unfamiliar seas. There have been times when crew morale has hit rock bottom as money problems and sickness grounded us. Sometimes I've felt like jumping overboard and we all entertained the idea of crew members walking the plank at times. I understand what it means to "sail heavy seas with a torn mainsail" or to function when weighed down with wet-weather gear. As James Michener said in his book *Chesapeake*...

"A ship, like a human being, moves best when it is slightly athwart the wind, when it has to keep its sails tight and attend its course. Ships, like men, do poorly when the wind is directly behind, pushing them sloppily on their way so that no care is required in steering or in management of sails; the wind seems favourable, for it blows in the direction one is heading, but actually it is destructive because it induces a relaxation in tension and skill.

"What is needed is a wind slightly opposed to the ship, for then tension can be maintained, and juices can flow, and ideas can germinate; for ships, like men, respond to challenge."

I took a leaf from Michael Fay's book; he saw the America's Cup challenge as the "hardest thing around to do". I think we all need to be challenged and to launch out of our comfort zone. Otherwise nothing can be achieved.

I realised I didn't have his money or clout, the sailing skills of this elite team, or "the hype and glory of the challenge". Even so, I hoisted my mainsail and launched into whatever life threw at me. Around this time, wisdom turned up in these pieces of advice from Noah's Ark:

Don't miss the boat.
Remember that we are all in the same boat.
Plan ahead. It wasn't raining when Noah built the Ark.
Stay fit. When you're sixty years old, someone may ask you

to do something really big.

Don't listen to critics; just get on with the job that needs to be done.

Build your future on high ground.

For safety's sake, travel in pairs.

Speed isn't always an advantage. The snails were on board with the cheetahs.

When you're stressed, float awhile. Remember, the Ark was built by amateurs; the Titanic by professionals.

No matter the storm, there's always a rainbow waiting.

※ ※ ※

I would add that when embarking on any journey, it's good to choose your travel companions wisely. I can imagine the Ark was smelly, and after forty days and nights the aggressive grumpy animals would've been pretty hard to live with.

There we go, sometimes old wisdom is the best. Happy sailing.

18

Christmas was a challenge for me, trying to normalize the celebration with an absentee father and a non-existent husband.

I felt deeply the "Noah's Ark syndrome" as two-by-two, families shopped and ate and had real holidays together. The happiness of the children buoyed my spirits as we decorated the small tree and handmade decorations. We made popcorn cakes and fudge and read the Christmas story before opening our modest presents. It was at this time of the year that I felt the most lonely and vulnerable.

It took me a while to see that no family is perfect...

Broken Families

A few years ago, I visited South America.

Apart from the fabulous scenery and wonderful sights, I spent considerable time in quaint markets. They were everywhere—on hillsides suspended in the Andes, in crowded cities, and in tranquil valleys.

On our last day in Chile we visited an up-market shop dripping with lapis lazuli jewelry and other souvenirs way out of my price range. I did, however, find a beautifully crafted nativity set in terracotta.

There's Mary and Joseph and baby Jesus in a crude cradle. I purchased a cute grey donkey, a dirty sheep, and a baby alpaca to complete the happy family—'cos everybody knows there were alpacas at the birth of Jesus! The shop assistant wrapped it in bubble-wrap and I carefully carried it home.

I was so upset to find when I unwrapped it, that Joseph was cracked in the head. The perfect family no longer existed. Mary was on her own, a solo mother with a child and a stable full of stinky animals.

For a lot of people, Christmas brings huge stresses—lack of money, lack of time and unrealistic expectations of happiness.

Many Marys struggle to raise children alone and lots of broken Josephs also are separated from their children, sometimes not from choice.

I pulled myself together, glued Joseph's cracked cranium and did the best I could.

As I meditated on the idea that Christmas is not a bunch of fluffy ducks, my thoughts transported me back to the first Christmas...

Mary Christmas

A couple of years ago I was given tickets to the movie *The Nativity Story* and went, thinking it would probably be some Hollywood-hyped up affair.

But it wasn't. It showed all the wonder and grace of the Christmas story but also showed the reality of life under harsh Roman rule. Mary and Joseph didn't have it easy either.

Their community for the most part didn't want them—a young girl pregnant and unmarried was hardly going to be voted Mother of the Year.

Imagine Joseph trying to explain to his mates that his potential bride was pregnant by the Holy Spirit—and carrying the Son of God to boot. The carpenters' workshop would no doubt have been abuzz with sniggering innuendo. And Mary's parents would also have struggled to accept her role in the greatest story ever told.

To be honest, some Christmases have been less than ideal, and I share that experience with many people. It's not easy if you're alone, or a single mother, or struggling with illness or financial worries.

In the end both Mary and Joseph coped because they were believers... in their God and in each other.

Now, if I'd been God, I would've done Christmas differently.

For a start I would've hired a decent PR firm with me in charge. I mean it all seems a bit understated to me—a teenage girl chosen from an ordinary home to give birth to the son of God. There wasn't even a nationwide search with auditions like in X-Factor.

And I'd have chosen a famous star for the job—maybe a Britney Spears or a Taylor Swift, for goodness sake. Just imagine the media frenzy, the Press would've been all over Bethlehem like a rash, dying to get the first pictures.

The build-up to the great event could've been handled much better also. Britney could bring out a new range of maternity wear, perhaps some cool hipster pants and a midriff top printed with the words "Are you Ready to Meet your God" or something else equally clever. I'd have produced a documentary called *The Immaculate Conception...the Real Story.*

Then there's potential in that poor little donkey, trudging through the snow, maybe getting lame and barely making it to the stable. The cameras could record its last desperate hee-haws. Can you imagine the public outrage? Donkey food manufacturers would be all over that one.

Think of the marketing mileage in the three wise men! Sales of frankincense and myrrh would've gone through the roof. I'm sure a new men's clothing line could be launched. After all, those dudes were pretty exotic. Fancy hats and Aladdin-type shoes with curly toes would become du jour.

Just think what Trip Adviser could do with the reviews of the accommodation. "Cosy, warm, bijou room available, complete with comfy bedding. A refreshing alternative to those large, soulless hotels. Pet friendly."

But God had other plans. He dropped into the world virtually unannounced. Just the few wise men, a handful of shepherds, a husband and a few farm animals, were witnesses to the greatest show on earth, and the only obvious big star was in the sky.

Yea, I'd have done it differently, but I wasn't asked, and I can't save the world.

19

Meanwhile, back at the coalface

I remember, one night, sobbing in my room after a big letdown by a friend. One of my daughters popped her head around the door and said she had an urgent question.

"How long can sperm survive in the outside air?"

That pulled me out of the ugly cry, and I was relieved to find the information was not needed by her. That morphed into an interesting discussion about the birds and the bees.

One can't be too sure, however.

The Rat Race

On Mother's Day, I feel the need to confess my sins.

You see, I haven't been a perfect mother. My children are now grown up and I've survived with my sanity almost intact. There were times when I loved them to bits and other times when I wanted to chop them into bits and flush them down the toilet. The only thing that stopped me was the effect on the plumbing bill.

At times a long jail term with meals provided looked rather attractive.

I've been sad, mad, overreactive, too soft and too hard. I do remember a brief period of ecstasy… for about five minutes after they were born.

My children were part of a risky experiment and I was the scientist. I understand that these days they have computerized virtual rats and guinea pigs to do their tests on, but my poor children were the real thing.

My youngest had a love affair with rats. She brought them home from Kindy for the holidays. She told me once that she loved them so much, she'd kissed them on the lips.

Her rats reminded me of the worst kind of teenager. They smelt bad, ate like horses, and were always trying to reproduce. Later we talked more about the dangers of kissing human rats on the lips.

But this Mother's Day I'll look at my four wonderful children, my heart will burst with love and pride, and I'll thank God for each one of them.

Times have changed in parenting and one difference is this:

In my parenting days, I would buy some disinfectant, a bath cleaner and a bottle of bleach. When the kids were babies, I had muslin cloths for their faces and their bottoms and ripped-up nappies for vomit catchers. Now there are special wipes (throw away of course) and a nappy bag full of creams and potions to keep baby pristine and non-stinking. At all costs the public must never know that babies have bodily functions—at least not ones that can't be masked in an artificial scent.

For the house, there are cleaners for the bathroom, different cleaners for the kitchen, lemon scented floor wipes, and scented garbage bags. A spray-on shower cleaner promises you'll never have to scrub again. This little breakthrough in hygiene only costs five times the price of a basic cleaner. Tissues are immersed in aloe-vera or eucalyptus, and toilet paper with lavender or gardenia. As for the toilet, cleaners are coloured blue to make it look like the tranquil waters of the Pacific. If that isn't enough, you can buy a toilet duck to go around the bend on your behalf.

I remember as a child, my Mum carried a supply which is now out of fashion. She had an almost inexhaustible supply of spit. I've carried on the legacy. Honestly, it can clean just about anything.

The Long Haul

Sometimes I'm invited to speak about my experiences as a single parent. I start by telling my audience that I'm not an expert but rather a fellow survivor. While raising my four children, I ran the gamut of every emotion including periods of utter desperation.

My children had strong personalities and developing character was all about consistency. Sometimes they terrified me with their demands, and I gave in for the sake of peace. Most of the time I was just too exhausted to resist.

The writer, Chekov, summed it up in a sentence. He said, "Any idiot can face a crisis. It's the day-to-day living that wears you out."

I tell the tired souls whom I address that parenting is a marathon. I'm informed that a marathon runner counts the number of strides he takes to finish the race, mentally checking them off to encourage himself to keep going when his body and mind have almost given up.

It's amazing that raising children can push you to the edge, yet also be the reason to survive and succeed.

It is the most important job in the world and for me it's been extremely fulfilling. So, this one's for my kids. Thanks for still loving me, and thanks for turning out so well... in spite of me.

It's all so cute when they're first born—that downy, warm head nuzzling at the breast. The emotion as you look at your child is overwhelming. Then they get older and the stages between baby and adulthood can be rather daunting. The trick is to never let them see your terror and rigorously defend your right to incompetency.

With a lot of soul-searching and agonizing, we see our children sowing their wild oats, rebelling against family values, and generally being right pains.

Never underestimate the power of consistent training and input into our children.

I heard a story the other day that gave me hope.

A little boy ran away from home on his bicycle. A neighbour noticed him at the end of the street riding round and around in circles on the grass verge. He stopped and asked the boy what he was up to and the boy told him that he was running away. The neighbour commented that he hadn't gone very far and asked him why.

"Well," said the boy, "my Mum always told me I'm not allowed to cross the street on my bicycle." So much for the grand getaway.

Parenting is never smooth sailing. One friend described it as "like being pecked to death by a duck". But we must never give up because it's the most important job in the world.

A neighbour told me she'd been served a wonderful breakfast of fruit and cornflakes topped with mayonnaise on Mother's Day because they'd run out of yoghurt.

I know for many Mums it's a difficult day because their children may not have walked an easy path. As Mums we need to quell the panic at times. Just because your children voice their disapproval doesn't mean they're going to hell in a bread basket. There were times when my children didn't like me very much and I have to say I returned the favour. You hear things that make your hair curl and turn grey; but the trick is to keep your eyebrows neutral and get on with the job.

A big challenge for singletons is Mother's Day, especially when your children live far away, and you face the day alone. I've found the best way to cope is to plan the day as though no better offer will turn up and then get on with it.

I walk to church in the morning with a slightly wobbly but buoyant heart and immerse myself in the inclusive and beautiful service. Coffee and chats follow with me carefully avoiding a straight answer about my plans for the day. Wobbly hearts can't cope with being tacked onto someone's plans as an afterthought.

Home to poached eggs on toast and only ten more hours to go, punctuated by the arrival of a bouquet of flowers from daughter-who-remembers-and-does-something. A couple of Skypes from other offspring pulls wobbly heart back.

I then set off for a long walk along the beach.

"How wonderful," wobbly heart reminds me as I watch multi-generational families enjoying their special day together.

"OK. What's next?" whispers the sensible person in my head.

"How about an ice cream?" I suggest, and wobbly heart agrees.

I walk the extra ten minutes to the ice cream shop only to be told that their Eftpos machine is broken and the forty cents in my purse would not suffice.

Honestly, officer, I didn't mean to stab the server, but he was mocking my pathetic lack of company, wasn't he?

Pulling sensible person and unhinged-by-this-stage wobbly heart together I walk back to town and find another source of ice cream. By the time I get home I have re-established my equilibrium and enjoy the rest of the day with a good book and a funny movie.

Next morning, I decide crying after Mother's Day was totally acceptable, so I burst into tears, bawling my eyes out, and then get on with my life.

Millions of parenting strides later, the finishing line was in sight.

20

Raising Mum

Although I loved raising them, part of me yelled "Hallelujah" when the last one married and my hands-on job finished.

One of the biggest lessons I learned while parenting was that children have a unique way of seeing through all your weaknesses. Mine, anyway, taught me early on that my behavior had to match up with my words or they'd point out my hypocrisy.

As one writer put it, "If you don't live it, they won't listen to it."

I may have had the illusion that I was teaching them valuable life skills, but my kids also taught me a lot.

I learned I could survive on minimal sleep. I once calculated that I'd had almost five years without an uninterrupted slumber. They've taught me that I can be pushed past the limits of human patience and not commit murder.

I learned that hugs are more important than wealth (although a bit more money never goes astray!)

They taught me to never covet a TV program because once they'd watched their choice (only one hour a day each) it was way past my bedtime. One of my children blames her TV addiction on my cruel, restrictive watching limitations.

And they taught me to eat and even enjoy leftovers. To this day I'm still crazy about cold toast. Crusts are delicious smeared with peanut butter, or jam, or marmite. Even now, when I can afford to eat whatever I like, I still eye up the leftovers on my fellow diners' plates at restaurants.

They taught me to deal with defiance, rejection, heartbreak and adolescence. My sales success developed while negotiating with four teenagers. If anybody practised free speech it was they, and for reasons that baffle me I have reproduced a clutch of offspring who can't wait to tell me what they really think.

They brought me down to size when I got too big for my boots. They reminded me of my parental responsibilities when I wanted to act like a teenager. They screamed 'hypocrisy' when I said one thing and did another. They exposed my weaknesses when they behaved just like I did and embarrassed me in front of my adoring public.

They checked up on me if I stayed out too late or failed to return their phone calls. Their health fads resulted in my liver being cleansed, my weight being monitored, and my carbs diminished. I've become an overnight success after thirty years of negotiation under my parenting black belt. I've been humiliated into gym attendance and shamed into higher learning.

I hope they never find out how much I really owe them because, so far, my education has cost me a fortune.

Then there was the shower story.

All Washed Up

My then twenty-year-old baby (the artist in our family) spelled out the words "I love you Mum", in dental floss on the shower wall.

I suspected she couldn't be bothered putting her used dental floss in the garbage, but that would be too petty on my part when the message was so sincere. This same girl has an easily-distracted personality which resulted in her wafting away from the dinner table, leaving her plate of half-eaten spag bol on the table on more than one occasion.

She was quite surprised one night when she retired to noddy-land and found her leftovers, plate and all, under the sheets at the foot of her bed.

* * *

Just when I graduated, my parenting marbles intact, grandchildren began to emerge, naked and blinking from their mothers' wombs.

I wondered if I had what it took to be a Grandma.

21

Trendy Grandma

I'm not a soppy, gaga sort of Grandma. I don't carry a brag book and bore everyone with detailed stories of my newest grandchild's bowel movements. Neither do I feel the need to spend all my money spoiling them. In fact, I've wondered if I'd ever get a handle on this Grandma stuff.

You see, I'm a trendy Grandma with a life of my own. I travel regularly, read all sorts of literature and try to keep up with what's cool in the music department. I hang out quite regularly at an inner-city bookshop, poking through the bookshelves and listening to music.

One day my daughter, nine months' pregnant, invited me to the bookshop for coffee and a good browse. Something happened inside me then that bordered on a spiritual experience.

After my usual tour of the travel section, sampling a little Latin salsa in the musical department, I meandered to the baby-and-child section to chat with my daughter.

She was surrounded by books on how to raise a happy baby. From the corner of my eye I saw a brightly-coloured book with animals portrayed on the cover. I picked it up, opened it, and was hooked. It was a pop-up book with lions and pandas and butterflies leaping out of the pages. I glanced at my daughter, flooded with gratitude. I realized then that I had what it took to be a real Grandma. Of course, I bought the book.

Remote Control

When your grandchildren live overseas you find creative ways of keeping in touch. My job was made a little easier with the introduction of Skype. I tried having a conversation with Amanda in Doha. She had three gorgeous girls, the youngest only six weeks old.

Little Miss eighteen-month-old had memorised the Skype signal. As soon as it rang, she raced to the computer. Mum was breastfeeding the baby with the laptop teetering on the arm of the couch. When the toddler realised it was me on the screen, she rushed to the playroom to gather an assortment of toys and books. Teddies and dolls and soft toys galore were paraded in front of the camera and I was expected to approve each and every one. Then she demanded I sing a nursery rhyme. Her big sister arrived on screen to show off her new glasses, by which time toddler had settled in to the new baby-bouncer and almost flattened it.

It is only then I get to talk to Amanda. This is hilarious as she must give directions to the kids in between short bursts of conversation. On this occasion she had to get big sister to wrest a screwdriver out of the toddler's hands so the Swiss ball would not be punctured. Toddler did not take this well. Somehow, we managed to cobble together enough conversation to find out we were both alive and kicking, and that was about it.

Finally, we gave up with a promise to try again tomorrow.

Melodies of Life

I sat with one sick granddaughter watching a music DVD. I don't often sit for two hours but she snuggled on my lap, sucking her sipper-cup, dozing off. The DVD was a kiddy music show which included amazing little songs that conveyed messages about sharing.

Music is incredible. Think about all the words that have been written and the millions of tunes created through the centuries.

As I cuddled this wee girl with her mass of Shirley Temple curls, it occurred to me that she is also a walking, talking, song in progress. She has her own rhythm, her own words to impact her world, and her own songs to sing. Some of her songs will no doubt be a bit sad, some full of joy, as life hands out its inevitable mixture of trials and happiness. There'll also be humourous songs, passionate songs and songs of protest. Her musical DNA has already been written and it will be exciting to see how she fits into our family song album.

As I pondered over this, she opened her sleepy eyes and snuggled closer. I sang a lullaby to help her feel safe and to get her through her sickness. I realised then that I also am part of her life song. That felt really great.

California called to check in with the American family branch.

Mummy

I'd been staying with Emily to help with the children... and the housework... and the cooking... and the laundry.

Although she's been married for nine years, she seems to revert to childhood as soon as I walk in the door. You see, she's a laid-back dreamer. All she ever wanted was peace. And then came children. These kids never stopped moving from sun-up to sun-down.

Emily remembers the first day they said "Mummy" and the joy that brought to her heart. Now every phone call, every email, and every bowel motion is punctuated by that one word—over and over again.

She is ripped from her slumber at ungodly hours in the night. The next day they punish her with grumpy behaviour for getting up to soothe them.

It would be the understatement of the year to say her adorable, twenty-month-old little boy, Ezra, was busy. Table tops were his favourite playground, together with kitchen benches, armchairs, and the backs of couches from which he launched himself with no fear at all—usually with no clothes on. You haven't lived until a small nude bottom catapults on to your head while you are minding your own business.

My computer has been denuded of the O key and, as his mum vacuums, he felt the need to scatter foodstuffs in her path just for fun. Our only comfort was that his big sister had once been the same; with good parenting and the passing of time, she became very well-behaved—most of the time.

In the States they have subdivisions with large gates and a guard house. These gated communities provide security for the inhabitants and keep all danger out. Little did I know that I was about to experience a similar set-up at her house. Emily's house is like gated community. Thankfully, Ezra hasn't yet been able to figure out the mechanism which opens the gates. It kept me supple, hurdling the gates, but it kept me safe from the pint-sized boy who thought it fun to leap on me from great heights. If you ever get to visit my daughter remember my warning... step away from the gates.

Now it was time to visit my Antipodean son, Richard, and his family in Sydney.

Marathon Parenting

They had an adorable toddler named Georgia who could charm the whiskers off a kitten (that's if pulling them off doesn't work). She managed to keep three adults entertained and occupied for a full five days.

An encounter with a cupcake resulted in an extra, small load of laundry and a full high-chair clean-up.

Her soft toys were repeatedly bathed in the sandpit, then shaken out on to the carpet, unless we got there first. She learned to let her carers know when a nappy change was imminent by uttering the word "bum" in a big loud voice just as the aroma reached their nostrils—a good argument for teaching babies sign language. She also has a designated rubbish bin for her nappies.

Before we arrived, her Mum had cooked and pureed tons of vegetables to make sure she had a balanced diet—with some left over for the baby as well.

Although I'd raised four children, I'd forgotten how much work and patience and commitment are involved. Parenting is indeed a marathon.

It's the hardest job in the world and how much we enjoy it

comes down to our expectations of ourselves and our children. The most wonderful and the most terrifying thing about raising children is that they will, to some extent, turn out like you and if they don't, you blame the other parent. As a wise person said, "If they turn out like little angels, we shouldn't take all the credit. And if they don't turn out so well, we shouldn't take all the blame."

Nevertheless, it has been my observation that mothers especially are primarily motivated by guilt. There's Catholic guilt and Protestant guilt and Jewish guilt. There's false guilt and genuine guilt, although the latter is harder to come by. The biggest guilt trip of all is single-mother guilt where failure in relationships is added to the pile. The absent-parent guilt is rarely borne by the absent parent while the on-the-spot parent tries desperately to compensate. It's a futile exercise, and you may as well just go buy a hair-shirt and at least know for sure it's self-inflicted.

● ● ●

Speaking of self-flagellation…

22

In my travels I come across interesting but useless bits of information.

In Portugal for instance, I learnt a lot about Henry the Navigator, a member of the royal family and a devout Catholic. To keep his baser nature under control, he wore a hair shirt, which obviously caused great discomfort and made him more pious. That wouldn't work for me. I'm sure I was destined for silk and cashmere although my budget won't allow it.

I know that life implies suffering even if I don't go looking for it. Most of the time, trying to short-circuit the process causes more trouble than it's worth.

A man found a chrysalis suspended from a tree in his greenhouse. He watched the butterfly inside struggling to release itself from its prison. So, he decided to give it a hand. With a small scalpel he slit the chrysalis and the butterfly fell to the ground. He gently picked it up and put it on a shelf and went inside. The next morning, he found the butterfly dead. By stopping its struggle, he'd deprived it of the strength-building it needed to survive in the real world.

Every autumn, monarch butterflies migrate from the Eastern United States to several sites in Mexico. If born in August in New York, they fly all the way to Mexico, spend the winter there, then fly north, laying eggs on milkweed along the Gulf Coast in Texas and Florida before dying.

The butterflies born of those eggs continue the flight northward, breeding and laying more eggs along the way. By August, other monarchs, four generations or so removed from the butterflies which left New York for Mexico, will emerge from their chrysalises and repeat the journey. Heading south, they aim for a place they've never been to, a specific acre or two of forest on the steep slopes of a particular mountain range. It seems the circle of life can be very circuitous.

I'm grateful for my struggles. At least I've learnt not to take myself too seriously, to understand that bowls of cherries always have pits and that life is for living, warts and all.

Get them before they get you

Maybe it's because my children could see chinks in my armour that they repeatedly thought I needed instruction. Little did they know I was about to get my own back.

Poetic Justice

I was about to celebrate a significant birthday—the first one I'd celebrated without children living in my home. I suffered a bit of "empty nest syndrome" which brought about a real change in my thinking.

A week before my big day, my daughter asked what I wanted as a gift and was somewhat surprised when I said I would like a new electric blanket to replace the cheap one I had, which quite frankly had become a health hazard.

This time, I explained, I would like one with a sheepskin top so that the electrical wires don't scratch my back. To top it off I didn't want cheap artificial fleece. I wanted pure New Zealand wool.

They obviously had a conference about it because she came back to negotiate a compromise. It seems the kind I wanted came in well over budget.

"It's funny Mum", she said. "When I was four you said a sloppy kiss and a hug were all you needed. When I was eight you were delighted if I made something out of popsicle sticks. When I was fifteen, I could get by with the promise of doing extra chores or bringing you breakfast in bed. My, how times have changed."

In my deeper wisdom. I decided it was not the time to remind her of how much I'd forked out for four children and years of parenting.

So, on my birthday, when I opened my expensive and luxurious gift, I made sure they all got a sloppy kiss and a big hug.

Wisdom couched in reality kept arriving at my door. I had to admit that I was mediocrely talented in a few things, and perfectionism was not my strong point.

But it's been said that perfectionists take great pains and give them to others.

23

If a job's worth doing, it's worth doing well...or is it?

My Mum was in her nineties when I calculated she'd fed over 500,000 mouths during her lifetime as a cook. I don't remember her serving any meals from packets.

My women friends, on the other hand, are generally sick to death of cooking. Luckily for us, the market has recognised our ennui and provides many pre-prepared meals. My point is that, unless you're into haute cuisine, there are many things that are not necessarily worth doing well unless you adore doing them.

Boring tasks must be done faster and with less application to get to something more fun. Wisdom is finding out when you can get away with it.

For example, you won't find me anywhere near the toilet with a toothbrush. It's not worth it unless your husband has been difficult, and it's his toothbrush! Which segues conveniently into my toilet story.

Toiletries

I've achieved a few things in my short life. I'm reasonably literate, I've traveled a lot, often on my own, and I've raised four children, none of whom have turned out to be Texas axe murderers.

I've stayed out of jail, paid large middle-income taxes, never had an affair, or used tax-payers' money to finance my election campaign.

The fact that I've never run an election campaign is irrelevant… it's the principle that counts.

I once interviewed the Prime Minister for a short time, and when I lived in California my Avon lady knew Barry Manilow, or so she said. So, you can see I'm really quite important and deserve the respect that goes with my lofty reputation.

Unfortunately, my status doesn't seem to count at home and as a result I have unofficially and without my permission, been given the job of toilet-roll-holder refiller. I'm absolutely convinced that family members and visitors to my home hold meetings behind closed doors to conspire to measure the toilet paper so that it runs out just as nature calls me.

Sometimes I think I've beaten them when I gleefully see that there's just enough left. Alas my calculations are often in vain and once again I'm called to do my duty. I've even tried leaving it empty so that the next person has to fulfill the obligation. Guess who the next person usually is?

Some people are called to greatness and some have it thrust upon them. I've just learned to roll with it.

Laughter is the best medicine and my sides are splitting.

Flying Solo

I wonder if someone might start a Singles Anonymous for people like me who could stand up at meetings and say, "Hi, I'm Frances Hall and I'm single"—although I would no longer be anonymous.

I'm sure I would feel much better once I'd got it off my chest, so to speak.

Flying solo has its ups and downs. For me, one challenge is the lack of spontaneous conversation. I see a great TV show, or a spectacular sunset and I must absorb it alone. To top it off, I'm on a diet to shed some of the belly fat that could cause me to cark it.

I do have my faith intact though, so with all this in mind, I may write a book called "No eat, Pray, No Love", although I suspect it won't make it to the top of any bestseller lists.

Being me, and a bit outside-the-box, I'm always looking to alleviate my situation and put a positive spin on things. When I woke up feeling bereft of a hug one morning, I considered the options.

I thought I would get the big teddy bear from the spare room and shove him in the bed like a pseudo partner, but I suspect he'd be too big to take to the Rest Home in thirty years, should I become attached to him.

So instead I got up, called a friend, and went to the movies. If all else failed there was always my antique golliwog with one eye. *Ewwww!*

As I write this, I'm reminded of the golliwog left to me by a dear friend who died too early from cancer. She was an antiques nut and I was Thoroughly Modern Millie, but we still had great times together and I miss her a lot.

24

And yet I knew it would get better

I was forty-five and a full-time job beckoned.

Applying for jobs in the travel industry one day, I saw a position at Grapevine Magazine for an advertising sales rep. The salary was $13,000 with a car provided—rich pickings for me. I knew nothing about the job, but in my usual, bolshie way I turned up for an interview.

It was here that I met a man who would literally change my life. The editor, John Cooney, must've seen something of value in me and opened every opportunity he could find. I blossomed, achieving everything I could've dreamed of. I went from ad sales to Sales Manager and went back to University at night to do a Sales Management course.

He then suggested I have a crack at writing and assigned me to interview refugees in New Zealand and to write travel articles. Who would have thought that in my middle years I would become a bona fide writer?

Henry James said that a writer must be "one of the people on whom nothing is lost" and my curiosity was paying off.

I was approached to write and present radio scripts—slice-of-life type stories with spiritual and humourous twists. I loved this and wrote over eight hundred scripts during this career, some of which I've inflicted on you, my captive audience.

Then, to come full circle, I was asked to lead tours for a fledgling tour company, Tours Direct. My passion for travel and especially all things Spanish was finally being satisfied. Recently, my DNA test revealed that 8% of me is Iberian. My father had always said that we had Spanish blood...something about the Armada going down off the coast of England, the sailors swimming ashore—and the rest, as they say, is history.

I found myself in far-flung places—Easter Island, Peru, Morocco and Cuba. My heart soared listening to Spanish guitar music, and Andes pan flutes. You haven't lived until you've breakfasted on the Spanish Med, lunched in Tangiers, and dined on the Atlantic, all in one day.

So, back to study I went and spent two years bettering my *Español.* I am not fluent by any means but have learned to ask for things and then ask for the donor to just go get what I need without talking back, *por favor.*

Learning a language is one thing, using it is another.

Lost in Translation

Once, on a flight from La Paz to Santiago, I decided to engage the neighboring fellow passenger in conversation. I asked him about his family, and he returned the compliment.

Unfortunately, my words were a bit mixed up and, in my usual bull-at-a-gate fashion, I launched into conversation. Instead of saying I had four children, I told him I had four boyfriends; one in London, one in Toronto, one in America, and one in Auckland.

His eyes widened as big as millwheels. Fortunately, before he asked for an upgrade to first-class, I realized I'd made a boo-boo. We had a good laugh about it and I kept my mouth shut for the remainder of the flight.

I again felt the need to inflict my linguistic flair in a restaurant in Buenos Aires and confidently ordered from the menu. Shortly after, plate after plate of food arrived. It seems that my *ojos* were bigger than my *estomago*. I vaguely remember Miss Piggy saying we should never eat more than we can carry so I'll bear that in mind next time.

You can have a lot of fun when you're a foreigner. The day after the Miss Piggy episode I was in a food hall being very careful about my food choices. A local heard my bunglings and asked me where I was from. "Ah New Zealand!", he exclaimed. "All Blacks, kamate kamate."

A lot of Brits, Irish and Welsh people live in Argentina which is why it's the only South American country to have a major international rugby team. It's also the reason I was introduced to a gaucho called Pablo Flewellyn, and why Santiago's main street is named Bernardo O'Higgins Avenue after one of the founders of modern Chile.

Hysterics resulted when I tried to explain "rattle your dags" to a Chilean guide; it was even funnier when he tried to translate it to Spanish for the driver, who spoke no English.

I finally realized the effectiveness of my language studies when I successfully described a tour member's vomit to a doctor in Machu Picchu. (Just thought I'd bring that one up.)

High Jinx

When leading tour groups, among the various challenges were their health issues, especially when travelling overland at high altitudes. My repeated admonitions to eat small amounts and to drink little were often ignored; I can't blame them when yummy Pisco Sours are on tap. My advice did not stop one lady from almost falling in the fountain at a posh Peruvian hotel after imbibing two doubles on an empty stomach.

Climbing Machu Picchu is a challenge, and more so for someone with a throbbing hangover. She took one look at the ruins and gasped, "Are we supposed to climb up that?"

When staying in a posh hotel, another tour member needed help in finding relief for her hemorrhoids. She asked if I would go to the kitchen and ask the staff for a rubber glove. her plan was for the staff to cut one finger off the glove, fill it with water, and freeze it; then give the ice-in-glove-finger to her for her therapy. My mind and other anatomical parts boggled at that one. I suggested she get a bag of ice from the bar and sit on it.

Psst! Come closer, I have a secret. I am directionally dyslexic.

I feel better, now that I've confessed. Fortunately, we employ local guides in the countries we visit.

I've learned a little hack for tour guides. You will sometimes have one group member (usually a man) who thinks they could do your job better. I give that man a job. I ask him to get us safely to a local restaurant without getting lost. A man with a job is a joy and he will often become my support person for the rest of the tour.

Speaking of getting lost, I haven't lost a passenger yet... well, not for too long. Travel can teach us so much, if we let it.

Travelers not Tourists

I'd just returned from a wonderful trip through Spain, Portugal, and Morocco. There's a lot to be said for being bathed in balmy Mediterranean breezes for three weeks, and the absolute privilege has not eluded me.

I certainly haven't traveled enough to be blasé about it. I still wander wide-eyed and open-mouthed through historic places, and revel in stories of gallantry and horror.

I was somewhat surprised at the attitude of tourists on the same trail. They whinged and moaned about everything, sighing and gritting their teeth as the destinations failed to produce facilities cloned from their native countries. The food, the hotels, and especially the loos, were often a source of dissatisfaction.

I discussed this with a member of one group and he said, "Ah, yes. They are tourists, not travelers. They visit, view, and leave and take very little with them. They don't know how to relax and enjoy the journey."

So, instead of taking them around yet another Cathedral on the tour, I sat inside and thought about the millions of people who had prayed there. I wondered what may have been in their hearts at the time. I listened to the prayers of mums like me who sought answers for their children, just as I would've done.

Paul Theroux said, "…Places had voices that were not their own; they were backdrops to a greater drama, or else to something astonishingly ordinary…"

I concur. I sat on a step in Machu Picchu and stared into the primordial mist of the rain forest, my heart burdened, and my head spinning from my recent trauma.

In that place I began to unravel the abuse in my second marriage, to allow the mystery of these damaged but indestructible buildings to inform my own; I began the process to healing. In my own "Incan" way, when backed into a corner by a terrifying threat, forced to abandon my home, I sought safety.

But enough melancholy. I had so much to celebrate while clambering among the ruins and gazing across magnificent vistas. Here, the still small echoes of peace permeated my soul.

We climbed, and from the top of the ancient city we watched as a group of white-robed worshipers danced in a circle below. Later, I was told that this is where a spaceship once landed and were trying to make contact again. Aliens are part of popular culture in parts of South America. Their existence and their one-time presence on Earth is the local people's way of explaining some of the seriously impossible building structures and weird happenings in the region.

I glanced anxiously around for Klingons on the starboard bow but saw only a few haughty llamas munching away on the terraced gardens. Mind you, those llamas do look a bit out-of-this-world. Beam me up, Scottie.

I'm not holding my breath for an out-of-body experience. I suspect I'd come back to find me and my problems still intact, so I may as well get on with dealing with them on terra firma.

To me, this is what being a traveler really means. We need to touch the sides of the past, the present, and the future, and let life seep into our hearts and minds and make this privilege count.

Theroux said, "Although the journey was over, the experience wasn't."

Movies, documentaries, and other travelers' stories repeatedly lure me to dine out on the places and people I've encountered along the way. I recall Inca trail porters with their bandy legs, in sandals made from old tyres, running great distances at an altitude of 4000 metres, carrying over fifty kilos on their backs. Their barreled chests and rosy cheeks are the visible indicators of their adaptation to the altitude. Colourfully-clad women and children, in their best attire, woolen petticoated skirts and knitted hats, touted their wares along the tracks.

We rattled in our luxury train, a long way below the trail, watching the mountain rivers gush and trickle over large rocks, and terraced gardens marching up the mountains like horizontal soldiers holding their battle lines. Man is ingenious when adapting to his environment, survival being a powerful catalyst for invention.

One of the joys of my tour-leader gig is that I get to meet some wonderful colleagues. I'm privy to their wisdom, knowledge, and sometimes black humour as we share harrowing experiences. They always have amazing stories to tell.

Up a Creek

As I wandered through the spray of Iguazu Falls, through the haze of rainbow prisms, I asked the guide if she had been asked any strange questions by other tours.

She said, "One woman, on seeing the colours in the mist, said, 'I'm so happy for you that you now have rainbows in Brazil.' I replied, 'Yes, our economy has picked up and we've been able to buy some.'"

Another had asked her how they got the figure eight shape onto the butterflies' wings and she told her they collect them every morning and stamp their wings and let them go!

I saw a sign in Portuguese which, when translated, commanded—'Do not feed the fish'. I thought this was very sensible given the presence of piranhas in the river.

Travel is not without its trials and I wrote this story tongue-in-cheek after a particularly harrowing long-haul flight.

25

Fly-by-Night

The other day, I saw an ad for a course on how to overcome the fear of flying.

I don't know what they teach you, but I suspect they don't tell you the whole truth. Flying in a plane is dangerous. There are obvious perils like crashing or hijacking; but it's the little things that we need to be aware of.

Noise levels for one. Never sit next to a snorer. How many decibels can one person generate to drown out multiple jet engines plus Elvis Presley input directly into both ears?

It's a good idea to lay claim to a window seat as soon as you board. Chances are, though, that even if the plane is half-full that seat has been allocated and it ain't to you.

Never sit next to a very large person. You will resent the extra luggage surcharge you paid when you end up with only half a seat. He's usually the one next to you in the window seat. He invariably has bladder problems.

And what about that popping ear syndrome?

One passenger described it as an articulated truck backing up through her ear canals, trying not to touch the sides. She'd spent mega bucks to have an ear specialist check her hearing.

He said she had nothing wrong with her hearing. She replied, "What?"

Watch out for the earphones. They are strangulation devices, especially if you fail to disconnect them before going to the loo.

However, death-by-earphone is infinitely preferable to what could happen in an airplane toilet. The paper has usually run out. The sign above the taps warn that the water is not potable (which means it is riddled with germs). Unfortunately, it also gushes at random, probably drenching you in hepatitis C or bubonic plague.

That's if you survive the toileting experience. Remember to get *off* the loo before you flush. That sucking action is powered by the jet engines. The force is so great it is capable of sucking out all of your interior organs into the atmosphere, never to be seen again—except by a nomadic herdsman in Tibet who is praying for food and finds an awful lot of offal at his dispossal *(sp intentional)*.

If you are still in one piece, watch out for those utensils. Firstly, you may be given only a plastic knife which is incapable of dissecting jelly. For some reason, a good solid steel fork is at your disposal. This said fork would be capable of slaughtering an entire crew if put in the hands of the wrong person.

Yep, they won't tell you all this on the 'fear of flying' course. They'll lull you into false security and lure you onto the plane with trumped-up safety statistics.

"Thank you for flying Aeroperil. We're so glad you've survived... this time."

It isn't all bad though, especially when you get to go to Cuba.

Oh, the smells you will smell, the sights you will see, the music you'll hear, and the toes you will tap.

I came over all Dr Seussy as I landed in Havana, where a rickety baggage carousel eventually spewed out my luggage. We waited for ninety minutes while bale after bale of merchandise rotated. These had been flown in from Guyana via Panama City and evidently took priority over processing the tourists who will be buying them. This is the "chink in the armour" of communism—small businesses edging their way into the Cuban economy.

We sped through darkened streets (the effect of electricity shortages) and then plodded through goodness-knows-what, dragging our luggage to our casas *particulares* (AirBnBs) where the host hauled our bags with an antiquated pulley up three storeys.

This is a trip into a time warp. Chevrolets and Cadillacs are powered by Skoda motors. Colourful, lively people eke out their existence with such joy, probably lubricated to a large extent by an abundance of rum. The transport is ingenious with horse-drawn carriages, oxcarts, many Chinese cars (one of the few trading partners surviving after Mother Russia pulled the plug), and lots of rickshaws.

Cubans don't know what they don't know, and I found them an absolute joy - friendly, helpful, and always laughing. They have a "No. 8 wire" mentality—just like Kiwis—except they probably have no No. 8 wire!

The next morning, after a modest breakfast, we stepped blinking into the bright heat of Havana, to meet our guide who would introduce us to the captivating culture and history of Cuba.

In Havana, colour and chaos clamour for attention. Every corner reveals another decrepit building crawling with renovators. The architectural styles are eclectic—everything from colonial grandeur to art deco sun-burst stained glass, and even Moorish simplicity. Marble pillared hotels tower side-by-side with crumbled ruins.

Havana seeped into my heart and I was keen to experience the real back streets. Lucky for me our boutique hotel hangs over a narrow lane.

We lined up at a bank to convert our Euros into CUCs, watched carefully by a security guard. It didn't look like he was having much fun.

But we were, as we strolled through cobblestoned streets to the waterfront—'*Malecon*' as it's known. I'd asked reception for Wi-fi (or *weefee* in Spanish). She gave very specific instructions: turn left out of the hotel, walk exactly one hundred metres, cross the main highway carefully, sit on the seawall, and you'll get a signal. And she was right.

This is boy-racer territory. The demographic is older, but they still drive like maniacs.

Old American cars trawled the streets looking for fares. A beautiful '56 Bel Air powered by a Lada motor may be held together by string, but its faded glory was nostalgic. It was like being on the set of "Happy Days".

A bright red Cadillac zoomed past, the driver resplendent in a large cowboy hat as he puffed on a large cigar.

Dodging in and out between these beautiful relics are hundreds of cheap Chinese taxis. China is one of Cuba's trading partners and our guide bemoaned the fact that lots of cheap goods have flooded into Cuba to meet the needs of the burgeoning tourist trade.

A huge Italian cruise liner was moored at the dock. It towered incongruously over the waterfront, a predictor of Cuba's future.

Everywhere, monuments honoured their heroes, including the iconic Che Guevara, wearing his trademark beret and fatigues, gazing pensively into the distance. I have to admit that he was one good-looking dude. Just as an aside, the Che photo most famously reproduced worldwide has evidently made more money than any other image and is a marketer's dream, selling everything from revolutions to condoms. Huge sculptures and photos of Castro and Che Guevara dominate the squares of Havana. Their stories are very compelling.

Fidel Castro continues to be adored. *Hasta Siempre, Comandante* (Until Forever, Commander) is blazoned on billboards throughout Cuba.

We continued our tour past the famous Hotel Nacional - full of bullet holes—and to the Presidential Palace where Batista narrowly escaped the militant students' attack. Each story had heroes, depending on what side you were on at the time. Bullet holes in walls are big business in Cuba, regarded as badges of courage and a potential draw for tourist dollars.

Food was limited in variety, but rum was plentiful, and everything tasted better after a couple of *piña coladas* or *cuba libres*.

We wandered back to our lodgings. That night I sat on the rickety balcony, sipping a cool one, while drinking in the sights and sounds from the lane below. Hawkers called out to potential buyers, cafés touted for business, and everywhere I heard the strains of a Cuban beat. I closed my eyes and swayed to the evocative music; the sheer pleasure of the day was absorbed by my whole being.

● ● ●

After a fitful night's sleep, I awoke and stumbled to my balcony. A rooster crowed in broad daylight jolting me from my reverie. The compelling aroma of Cuban coffee wafted from below and my nostrils awoke.

In the street below my accommodation, I found a range of hairdressers, small art galleries, and cafés with uniformed waiters. The ever-present Cuban musicians, eking out a living with their world class acts, worked their craft in bars and along the street. Young men strutted their stuff, coiffed in Cristiano Ronaldo hairstyles. Rap music cut across the salsa beat.

This new Cuba, a *mestizo* (mixture) of despotism, denial and hope, was fueled by a violent past and a compelling future. The people are real mestizos and the ethnic mix makes them pretty spunky. Mongrel religions—Catholic mixed with voodoo—are widely practiced.

The architecture would be described in modern terms as "shabby chic"—the understatement of the year. Rickety balconies, suspended precariously from the walls of stunning colonial buildings, a man or a woman (or both) leaned against the rails while music pulsated from within. There wasn't a Health and Safety Inspector in sight—messy, chaotic, noisy and rebelliously Cuban.

As you wander along a back street, salsa music seeps through the walls. Every restaurant meal is accompanied by top-class bands meandering among the diners.

Our guide, Jorge, managed to get us tickets to the Buena Vista Social Club at a very cool venue in Havana. I danced for hours with a Mexican and didn't suffer at all—until the next day. Evidently my moves were videoed and probably sell for mega bucks in markets...or not.

There's a bitter-sweet pride in the revolution and also a sense that it is becoming irrelevant and cannot sustain a younger generation champing at the bit for Nikes and McDonalds. But I suspect that, when they're let loose on the world stage, they'll make a big splash.

Cuba is surprisingly big—1,250 kilometres long—and we travelled the length of it. The geography is impressive with a third of the island dominated by huge mountains. Some is scrappy, uncultivated land. As we drove along, we saw mango trees dripping with fruit. Much is beautiful, with rivers and waterfalls and abundant white-sanded beaches. You haven't lived until you've lounged on a Cuban beach sipping a piña colada, or a mojito, or a Cuba libre, or all three!

The flora and fauna are amazing. I don't know about you, but I love seeing new birds and flowers.

We enjoyed a guided tour through an extensive botanical garden led by a lecturer with a Masters' degree.

Education is free in Cuba but few jobs are available and one of the biggest exports is human capital. There are over 37,000 medical professionals serving overseas. I've heard it's an $8 billion windfall for the Cuban government.

But, as a temporary import, I wondered if I had something to offer Cuba.

As I wandered the grounds of our run-down Spanishesque hotel, I stopped to chat to Alexander, a young man hanging around the hotel grounds, probably hoping for a few CUCs to come his way. He showed me a plaque marking the spot where Christopher Columbus landed in Cuba and we chatted about the history of the town and what life held for a family like his.

I indicated that I would love to meet his family, and so off we went along the dirt road, past the shanties, the pigs, and the dogs, until he led me to his mother's house. It was one space, with rooms separated by curtains. A hose brought running water through the window.

The neighbours peered through the chain-link fence, wondering who this strange gringo woman was and why she was hanging out in their hood. Someone scuttled away to make coffee and we sat chatting for an hour or so, me with limited Spanish and them with almost non-existent English. Her three sons were all university-educated and unemployed, and she earned $12 per month.

After returning home, I received adoring letters telling me how much our encounter meant to them and what a blessing I'd been.

That same house was flattened by Hurricane Irma and they were moved to a dwelling with no front door and no bathroom. When I visited again two years later, the whole family was waiting outside the hotel for me with kisses and hugs. The next day the mother brought a chocolate cake for the whole group and gifts to take home to my children. It was so humbling.

I am pleased to say I have paid to have a bathroom put in their house but this pales in comparison with what she's given me out of her meagre resources. We now share emails which she sends from the local post office. I have made a lifetime friend and I'm grateful.

Green Toilets

As a tour leader you hope and pray every day that there won't be problems on the way. But some things you can't control, and I have to say the following story involved much weeping and gnashing of teeth on my part.

On our way to La Paz the bus came to a sudden stop. Camped in the middle of the road was a large group of disgruntled Bolivians protesting about a government initiative. I'm sure their cause was not without merit, but this, the only route to the city, was blocked.

The guide took me aside and whispered, "We're going to go off road." Bear in mind that this was a small bus and all our luggage was strapped to the roof.

So, off we went over the furrowed fields. Startled farmers and llamas leaped away on either side. After about thirty minutes, it was obvious that we were lost. The driver jumped out and made his way to the nearest mud hut to ask for directions, and we took this opportunity to rest our bone-shattered bodies.

When it became clear that this little detour could take some time, the toilet question reared its ugly head. This was the first time I had to be "pee monitor". It was ladies to the left and gents to the right. I bet they had bumper crops that year, fueled by our exotic Kiwi waste products.

In my fantasies I wondered what would happen if we didn't survive? Wouldn't our bones be fascinating relics when found by archeologists in five hundred years' time? I could almost hear them saying, "These are definitely pre-Incan".

We finally circumvented all protestors and reached the main road. I waited with bated breath for outrage from the tour members. But they loved it and saw it as a highlight of the tour. It was a real "whew!" moment.

Several tours of La Paz included such excitement as dodging into cafés or detouring via side streets to avoid being caught up in demonstrations which frequently erupted unannounced. We managed to survive the markets where top-shelf baby alpaca woolen goods were displayed alongside llama fetuses and witchy amulets sure to improve everything from your finances to your fecundity. The last thing I needed was more children, so I chose a new scarf; and I wouldn't let any man near me with a barge pole if I knew he had a llama fetus hanging around.

And it's not a good idea to make major purchases at an altitude of 4,200 metres when your brain is deprived of oxygen.

* * *

Back home, I concentrated on getting my house in order and wheeled-and-dealed my way into financial security, ending up with two houses and a stability I'd never known before.

But money isn't everything and I still had a lot to learn as I ventured into a social life.

26

Watch out for Loose Women and Tight Men

A friend persuaded me to go to a nightclub. Her plan was to pick up a guy and I was the stooge to give her agenda legitimacy. We sat at a table and were soon joined by a couple of men.

My friend was pretty stroppy and after the preliminary small talk, she asked them to buy her a drink. They refused. She must have been very thirsty because she left the table to find someone else to hit up for a drink. One of the men commented that my friend was very pushy, "Not a nice woman like you."

I felt very embarrassed, so I chatted cheerily for a while to make them feel better. The interesting thing was, even though I was "nice", they didn't offer me a drink either. I bought my own before dehydration set in and I may have been tempted to dance.

C'est la vie! I'm glad I wasn't the only one flailing around in untapped waters...

Computer Geek

The world has indeed become our computer oyster.

Like everything else, the Internet has its pitfalls. A friend of mine signed up with an Internet dating service and discovered how tricky it can be.

At first it was so exciting. Men appeared from everywhere. Lots of 'chats' followed, and, for a select group, email addresses were exchanged. The list was culled to the few most likely suspects, and the serious business began.

There was coffee and a walk in the park for two lucky survivors. My friend speaks German and was pleased to discover that one of the possible suitors did also. They began an email exchange in German. She told him how much she had enjoyed their date and then wrote a long letter. After reading it through she entered his email address and clicked 'Send'.

Imagine her horror when she realized she had sent it to the wrong man. Prompt damage control was vital. She emailed suitor number two and asked him to delete the email and hoped like crazy he couldn't speak German. He was very gracious and said that was fine and she breathed a sigh of relief.

I suspect he went straight on to Google Translator.

The Older Chook in an Empty Nest

Eventually I reached a milestone in my personal development. Emily, all twenty-one years of her, decided that her time with me was up. She had spent most of her energy over the last two decades training me for the realities of life on my own.

My first lesson in this process was to learn how to talk to myself. This became increasingly obvious, especially during my children's teenage years, when I realized that they weren't listening to a word I said.

Then came the harsh lesson of learning to feed myself. My

daughter had, incidentally, bypassed this lesson. If there was any hint that dinner would not be on the table - in keeping with her social engagements—she would find another food source (namely Burger King, McDonalds or Wendy's). So, I was left talking to myself and eating alone.

Next, she taught me how to dress myself.

Words like, "That outfit is too old-fashioned. It has to go."

I learned the value of education. Her upkeep was such that I needed to upskill fast to ensure that she didn't end up supporting me.

She taught me everything I know about negotiation because nearly all my possessions had been used or retained by her and occasionally, I had to talk fast to get them back.

Finally, I've been toilet trained. I've cleaned every inch of that room religiously for over twenty years.

You'd think that by now I'd be pleased to see the back of her but there's just one problem. I can't seem to learn how not to be a mum. As the children got older and made their way in life, I had a mini crisis. Especially when my baby left the country in search of adventure.

The lead-up to this occasion was difficult. A round of parties and she was on such a high. I tried hard to celebrate. I felt nostalgic when I discovered all the junk she'd stored at home. I cried because I'd miss her even if her airfare was on my credit card and I was going to have to sell her car to pay for it.

I found myself giving her a crash course in Travel 101, feeling I only had one more chance to teach her what she needed to know. "It's a jungle out there!" "Don't go out with strange men!" "Keep your tickets and money separate!" and blah, blah, blah.

As I lined up with her at the check-in counter, I was still hard at it, fussing like an old mother hen. Finally, the man behind us in the queue had had enough. He leaned forward and gently said, "It's time to let her go."

My daughter turned and smiled gratefully at him. I nodded. He was right.

After some tears and lots of hugs, she walked through the departure gate and set off on her new journey.

I drove home to my empty house and wondered what the future held.

I was only fifty and a longing for intimacy began to gnaw. A quote from *The Lacuna* by Barbara Kingsolver no longer shored up my romantic leanings.

"What was my childhood disease? Love, I suppose. I was susceptible to contracting great love, suffering the chills and delirium of that pox. It seems I am safe now—unlikely to contract it again. People contort themselves to avoid the terror of being alone, making any compromise against it. It's a great freedom to give up on love and get on with everything else."

Given the success that I'd enjoyed, you'd think it would be enough. But loneliness became a constant condition, and me being me, it led to action.

27

Iwas aware my curiosity could be hazardous, but it didn't stop me dipping my paws in the waters of romantic illusion.

Inner Beauty

A perk of being a writer is you can investigate all sorts of dubious topics and call it "research".

Thus, I found myself researching the Dating Column in the local newspaper. Now this is the "noughties" isn't it, when new age appreciation for the inner person is paramount?

Yet the ads defied this attractive indicator of progress. First, a would-be Romeo builds the dreams of the hopeful reader to a frenzy of possibilities by listing wonderful, romantic options available—like walks on the beach, quiet dinners in cozy restaurants or beside a roaring fire, world travel, laughter... and happily-ever-after.

Just when the reader thinks she is a candidate for the shortlist, she's brought down to earth with a crash. Mr Wonderful has decided that he can only perform all these irresistible feats for a financially secure and - here's the clincher - a slim woman. Now what was he thinking? Perhaps that a chubbier woman is less likely to be financially secure, having chewed through her nest egg, and being now poised to have a go at his considerable assets?

I've heard that many men who put the "slim factor" in their ads are substantially overweight themselves, which means that some women at least are prepared to give inner beauty a chance to surface. Beauty may only be skin deep, but it is still a popular notion. I couldn't complete my research without going through the whole process, could I?

A couple of coffee dates evolved, with one likely man arriving at the café with a bunch of service-station flowers, well past their use-by-date. They died before the coffee arrived. I made my escape as soon as was humanly possible, but he followed me to the car, convinced that I was the love of his life. That episode did not end well.

Another date turned out to be the ex-fiancé of a good friend. It seemed the gene pool for this project was pretty shallow. Although I did discover another facet to my friend.

When I was first single, I had a long list of requirements for potential mates. As the years dragged on, the list became increasingly truncated until one day I confessed to a friend that breathing had become the only item in the line-up.

Time for a new strategy, I thought. So, I went to ballroom dancing evenings, kidding myself that it was for the joy of dance, but, from the corner of my eye, I was on the prowl.

The Last Waltz

Singles' dances take you back to those awkward teenage years when you lined up along the walls in your best frock and high heels, waiting for a likely lad to sweep you off your feet—or stomp your feet to shreds.

In later life the rituals continued. Some dances even had a glitter ball! Women gathered in small groups, surveying the talent and wondered if they'd be selected. It was poignant, with a touch of pathos rolled into one. The music is the same—lovely, lilting waltzes by Jim Reeves and Frank Sinatra, rock'n'roll with Elvis and Bill Haley, and a touch of Latin from Richie Valens. Throw in *Achy Breaky Heart* for the line-dancing, and we're all good to go.

It often struck me as somewhat cruel to put a group of lonely, single people in a slightly darkened room with a fifties' version of strobe lighting, romantic music playing, all thinking they'll escape unscathed.

If you love ballroom dancing, you must bear the awkwardness. Someone described this luscious form of torture as a "vertical expression of a horizontal desire".

Now of course I wasn't going to get sucked into this nonsense, I was there for the exercise!

The band launched into a romantic ballad, the singer crooned *Could I have this dance for the rest of my life, will you be my partner every night?* and several hundred singles glided on to the floor.

The air crackled with anticipation, a hint of desperation, and a substantial dollop of unadulterated lust.

I walked across the room and plonked myself next to a pert, spiked-coiffured redhead and waited for action.

After a few minutes, a somewhat diffident man approached Ms Redhead and asked if he could sit next to her. The look she gave him could have cut concrete and his sojourn was brief.

After he scuttled off with his tail between his legs, she explained that he was her ex-boyfriend and she'd just given him the flick.

My journalistic antennae beeped. I sensed a story, but before I could get to the nub of the issue, another prospect swept her to the floor and a frenzied rock 'n' roll set left her glowing.

She returned and sat down and said. "That was my ex-boyfriend too; but he's been gone a lot longer."

Now it was my turn for a bit of a flutter. A rather handsome Irishman with a twinkle in his eye and in his toes, asked me to dance.

"I've seen you here before," he whispered, and proceeded to sing to me in a beautiful tenor voice. "Put your sweet lips a little closer to the phone," he crooned.

Thump, thump, thump beat my love-starved heart as I gazed into his hazel eyes, and my knees weakened. The dance ended and he introduced me to his friend, a non-dancer whose job it was to prop up the wall next to the supper room, with a cool beer in his hands and a cold heart in his chest.

I made conversation. "I don't dance," he said, looking mildly irritated, "and everybody asks why I stand here."

I hurriedly thought of something more exciting to discuss with this pillar of the dancing community.

"Would you like to marry me and have my babies," I said and giggled at the absurdity.

"Why don't you ask Irish?" he hissed, "He'd be a good breeder."

Realizing I'd probably done my dash with Mr Wall Prop, I turned to Mr Irish for reassurance. Unfortunately, he'd been snaffled from right under my nose, so I held my head high and strutted back to my seat. By this time an old friend had arrived, and we sat and commiserated about the lack of good men. All was not lost in my search for journalistic excellence because she also had a story to tell.

"I've met this fella," she said. "He's really nice and he's here tonight." Her voice lowered as she explained that they had to play it cool because he was about to break up with another woman and she was there as well. The air vibrated with hormones as they brushed past each other or their eyes met across a crowded room.

More dances ensued with Mr Irish, then coffee in the city. Phone numbers were exchanged, and my love life looked like it was on the up and up.

But I would play it cool. "I have a life," I told myself as the phone failed to ring. It was Christmas time—one of those seasons that are tough for singles. The animals all seem to go in two by two—what I've coined "the Noah's Ark syndrome".

Finally, Mr Irish called and we went on a couple of dates. Boy, were they romantic! A rollicking romp in the surf, followed by dinner in a little country restaurant and an evening stroll by the river. Watching a video, snuggled up on the couch, and a chaste kiss on the lips at the end of a perfect evening.

A few nights later, I slipped on my dancing shoes and headed back to the singles dance.

Mr Irish seemed to have had a short memory. I danced the night away but not in his arms. He'd had a better offer and spent the night whisking around with a long line of adoring women. I realized I was in trouble. The supper waltz and the

Monte Carlo came and went, and I felt physically ill. I hadn't been able to eat much for weeks and it was beginning to take its toll. Mr Irish sauntered over eventually, said goodnight and disappeared out the door with another woman.

The woman sitting next to me sniffed. "Well," she said "he seems to have assembled quite a harem. I see him here often. Always got one or two women on the go."

"Really," I squeaked, my heart pounding and leaping from one breast to the other. Cupid's arrow shot through my left ventricle, blood drained from my face and my knees wobbled.

I realized—as Julia Roberts so succinctly said in one of her movies "...deep down I was just a girl looking for a boy to love her."

Would I ever learn? Apparently not.

● ● ●

28

Body Fat Index

I'm an advertising agency's worst nightmare. I'm in the target market for many goods and, theoretically, I should be buying lots of useless stuff. I read voraciously, including most of the junk mail that comes through my letter box. Unfortunately for Mr Marketing Manager, I rarely buy the goods.

A while ago I received a flyer from an electronics company. They advertised an animated singing bird (I decided against that), a digital camera for less than $70 (well, maybe), and an intelligent pre-programmed TV remote (I flagged that away—I never buy anything more intelligent than me).

I was about to bin the flyer when my eye spied a product that exceeded my wildest dreams. It was a special set of scales that measured body fat.

Finally, the answer to life's most pressing and profound question! *How much blubber is attached to my aging skeleton?*

No longer would I have to guess what's happened to that delicious pizza or that yummy cheesecake. With pin-point accuracy, my new scales could deliver instant guilt. I could carry these scales to restaurants and weigh myself after the entrée or the main and tell immediately if I was allowed dessert.

I was almost swayed until I read the fine print. It said the scales measured up to 5% body fat. With sinking heart and rising cellulite, I realized I was no longer in the target market.

But wait there's more...

I became a senior citizen. Yippee! now I'm overweight *and* old. The icing on this accomplishment cake spread thickly when I visited my daughter, Emily. After discovering that I had a mildly fatty liver, she went into a Google frenzy looking for cures. One site suggested colonic irrigation with gallons of tepid water and a large hose. It sounded rather drastic.

An array of liver-cleansing diets sounded awful—sort of eye-of-newt-mixed-with-turmeric recipes. I guess the turmeric helped ease the pain from this cure.

Or I could buy a kit from the pharmacy and D.I.Y. This option sounded easier but, as my daughter was about to close the deal and seal my fate, she read the fine print which read—"Do not use any of these diets if you are over 65."

I collapsed on the couch and reached for my Pinot.

I reviewed diets I'd tried, recalling more failures than successes. One that seemed to work last year was a low-carb number recommended by Jennifer Anniston.

Imagine my horror when I read that she's no longer endorsing this regime. There she stands, pencil thin, telling all her devotees that she was wrong, that low-carbing may not even be healthy.

And, to top it all, she was still not married to what's-his-name. I guess he'd had trouble finding her for years because she's so thin. But I digress.

So now I was back to square one. My illusions shattered, I had to fall back on that tried and true formula for weight loss—a balanced diet and regular exercise.

After that, I wondered if I should call what's-his-name. You never know, he may be at a loose end.

To add insult to injury, I switched on my computer to discover it was Happy Single-awareness Day. What was I supposed to do with this juicy snippet of information? Lobby my local MP for a husband? Run around in circles until I fell over myself? Bawl my eyes out until I was beside myself?

Perhaps I could do something about it...

29

Just when I Thought it was Safe to go Back in the Water (cue—the theme from Jaws)

If I'd had any sense, I would've stayed on my own.

I was about to give up my dreams of ever having another relationship, when an attractive, charismatic man literally waltzed into my life. I ascribed amazing nobility and moral character to him, swept on a tide of Connie Francis songs.

He was exceptional because I loved him, and I could make everything right in his life. His flaws would be washed away in my adoration. In this unhinged state I did some strange things.

Tan Me Hide

I'm not one for extensive beauty regimes, but I decided to try an all-over, fake, spray-on body tan. What possessed me to subject myself to such humiliation?

I sauntered into the local beauty parlour. Pretty soon a very young, very slim beautician greeted me and ushered me into a private room. New-age whale music played quietly in the background as I slipped out of something comfortable. "You can wear your underwear if you like," she said, "or try our paper G-string for the all-over effect."

My Scottish blood pulsed to the surface. For the $50 all-inclusive price, I was going to have as much tan as possible.

I clambered into the G-string. Did I imagine it, or did the whale music get louder?

The only way to describe the process is that it was like being in a vertical, freezing-cold rotisserie, in front of a full-length mirror.

I held my arms up at right-angles to my body "to prevent streaking", slowly rotating while the beautician sprayed the magical potion. At one point, she stopped to refill the container—which had run empty at about sixty-five kilograms. Boy, did that make me feel good! Finally, as the whale music spouted its final crescendo, the job was done.

"It will all be revealed in twenty-four hours," the beautician promised.

I exited, slimy and cold, from the salon and went home to await my glorious tanned emergence. Unfortunately, my skin decided that it didn't like this process. I have never seen anything so hideous. I had white elbows, bright orange shins, brown riveleted thighs and great yellowish patches under my arms. Unbeknown to me, the G-string hadn't been in the right place and I had a substantial white line down my buttock.

The salon offered another treatment—free. They could fill in the gaps, join up the dots and if that failed, I could probably reduce the colour by bathing myself in a weak solution of bleach. I demanded my money back.

30

Before the wedding day

I decided to put to death my navy cotton nightshirt with a ripped neckline. A friend and I popped into the lingerie shop at the mall to look for a replacement.

"Does that come in extra-large?" I asked the very young and dangerously thin shop assistant.

I saw what she was thinking. "Not that large," was written all over her face. But I acquired a temporary reading disability and charged into the changing room with a great stack of gorgeous outfits.

Reality dealt me a cruel blow. The underwear word for "smalls" did not apply to me. I could hardly contain my disappointment, and neither could any of the unmentionables. I imagined the sales assistant, her fingers poised to speed-dial the appropriate number to summon Greenpeace, to transport me back to my pod in an unfashionable sling. I decided not to stick around for the Greenies to throw buckets of water over me while waiting for the forklift.

In hindsight it was a sign.

Despite several red flags we married on Valentine's Day.

After eight years of abuse and a breakdown, I ran for the hills.

I was devastated. I'd never experienced such amorous passion. But passion is not love and love is not enough to redeem another person. The wonderful feelings I'd enjoyed were slaughtered.

I returned to the default emotion—indifference.

I've never had a bad temper and rarely experienced white-hot anger. My weapon of constant positivity and humour failed me then. It's hard to beat someone around the head with a smile on your face. I resorted to tears. My sobs fell on deaf ears.

I came to detest my vulnerability. I should have hardened up years ago and confronted the more dominating men I'd encountered. I should've been more calculating, asking the hard questions like, "What was in it for me?"

I couldn't make this marriage work and I believed it was all my fault.

Ann Voskamp in her book, *The Broken Way,* makes this claim. "Not one thing in your life is more important than figuring out how to live in the face of unspoken pain."

My hurt screamed on the inside, tearing me around the edges of faith and peace. I ran from pillar to post, unable to process the awfulness of it all. I slept fitfully, waking to an adrenalin rush of panic and feeling unhinged.

She, who'd been so strong, had her heart asunder. She, the party girl, who thought everything held some light, groped in thick, cloying darkness.

As I flailed around, something precious in me died. At the time, I couldn't see any purpose or lesson in the dying.

I had still to learn that a grain of wheat must fall to the ground and break open before there can be a new beginning.

The tendency after such an awful event is to close your heart, bolt the doors, batten the hatches, and then move through life with a mighty shield of self-preservation.

Ann Voskamp again, "Hurt is a contagion. When one person hurts in a family, everyone aches. And this is always the choice: pain demands to be felt—or it will demand you feel nothing at all."

Anger Management

I'd been hurt before and thought I'd learned a thing or two.

I wept my eyes dry. Then I got mad. I thoroughly reviewed the history of my relationship with this person. After allowing my anger to germinate and fester I felt extremely self-righteous. It was obvious to me that he had no right to treat me like that! Why I was practically a saint—after all I'd done for him! I spun my halo with increasing intensity and felt good for a while. I plotted my revenge. I wouldn't be so available any longer. He'd never take me for granted again. He'd be taught a lesson.

But bitterness dug a pit into my soul.

My head pounded. My stomach churned. I felt miserable.

Fortunately, I remembered a wise person who said - talking about relationships—"Unforgiveness, is a form of self-abuse. It's like an acid that eats away the receptacle that contains it, like eating poison and hoping someone else will die."

In that instant, I made an attempt to sort it out. In true psycho-correctness, I approached the perpetrator and tried to be conciliatory.

I can't begin to describe the way in which I was told to pull my head in.

So, there I was, sitting alone, seething and hurt in my one-woman pity party.

What to do?

I realized I had choices. I could continue my resentment. I could come up with a thousand arguments to prove me right and justify my outrage. Or I could plot revenge—spread my story, get other people on board and influence the way they related to this person.

That'd teach him a good lesson. He had it coming, didn't he?

And then I remembered there was a better way.

I could choose to forgive.

As I pondered this, I came across a story of a woman who had been severely abused. When asked why she wasn't bitter and twisted about it she said, "I distinctly remember forgetting what they did to me. I will not let the past lay its clammy fingers on the rest of my life."

Wise words indeed.

Slowly, I clawed my way out of my stuckness and took baby-steps to some insight.

31

Pity Party

To be brutally pragmatic, I found that misery loves company, but it isn't mine.

My mum once shared this little pearl of wisdom. Many of her contemporaries grumbled at length about their current ailments. Everything is discussed, examined in detail and agonized over... from palpitations to polyps. In other words—when you ask how they are, they tell you!

When you live alone, conversations are precious, but most of us could do without this variety. Strangely, those who have the most reason to complain rarely do.

Mum didn't want to fall into the moaning category, so she decided, as a precaution, to allow herself the occasional half-hour for private self-pity.

A strange thing happened. When she sat down to have a good worry about herself, she found it very difficult. Just as she was on the brink of indulging in a good moan, other thoughts insisted on intruding. Things like...

- Watching her great-granddaughter take her first steps just yesterday;

- Enjoying a walk along the beach with her daughter, sharing irreverent laughs about the relatives;

- She remembered that the tomato plants needed watering;

- And how much she had enjoyed that duet on the radio—Willie Nelson and Norah Jones, an unusual combination, but what a treat!

She settled into her pity party only to have her canary burst into joyous song and ruin the whole thing. Finally, she gave up and made a mental note to try again the next day.

As I prayed for another restoration, I sensed God saying, "Are you kidding...again?"

How faith saturates my life is often a mystery to me. I guess I don't fit the mould of traditional holy people. I'm a God-botherer, constantly asking questions about how it works or doesn't work, at least in my observation. I envy people whose faith is settled and decided and sure, 'cos I often wobble on the ledges of unbelief.

But there is one thing I'm sure of...

- Faith gives everybody a second chance;

- It undoes the damage life's challenges and trauma does to our hearts;

- Faith brings something out of nothing, turns desperation to hope;

- It brings perspective to every circumstance, chops up my ego and neutralizes my addiction to me.

The downside is that I must accept that I am not the be-all and end-all of the universe. Herein lies the rub. Faith commands that I forgive others and forgive myself. It demands personal responsibility. "The devil, my husband, my boss, my children made me do it" goes up in flames. As Judge Judy says, "All the shoulda-woulda-couldas are silenced."

Failure is never final when faith is invited. I can wake up tomorrow and know that there's power and possibility in each new day. Love, joy, and peace are up for grabs, and I need all I can get.

It was time for me to be quiet (a miracle in itself) and put my ears on.

Wisdom knocked on my door once more...

32

Listen, because I have important things to say, and what I tell you is right. What I say is true. I refuse to speak evil. Everything I say is honest; nothing I say is crooked or false.

People with good sense know what I say is true and those with knowledge know my words are right.

Choose my teachings instead of silver and knowledge rather than the finest gold.

Wisdom is more precious than rubies; nothing you could want is equal to it.

I am wisdom and I have good judgement. I also have knowledge and good sense.

Proverbs 8:6-11

C. S. Lewis said, "... pain insists upon being attended to. God whispers to us in our pleasures, speaks in our conscience, but shouts in our *pains*: it is his *megaphone* to rouse a deaf world."

Gentle voices gradually seeped back into my battered soul. It took several years for me to get my head above water and to recover mentally, emotionally and financially from my folly.

The story below says it all...

Blooming Good

When I fled an abusive marriage, part of the wrench was being uprooted from a beautiful home that my husband and I had built together

Luckily for me, friends took me in and nurtured me back to some semblance of normality. It took ages to recover and to lose the feeling that I'd been dug up and transplanted to a place not of my choosing. I felt I hovered in a parallel universe where nothing was as it seemed. Peoples' lives continued around me, but I was disconnected.

Life returned to a different 'normal' that was a bit scary. Financially, I'd taken a big hit, so a downtrodden house became my next project. Ripping parts of it to shreds was very cathartic as the renovation transformed it. The house functioned better and looked better and, bit by bit, so did I.

One very special joy was in the garden, a rose called *Double Delight*—irony screaming from heaven? I watered it daily and, when it bloomed, I'd breathe in its wonderful scent. It had obviously been planted when the house was built as its gnarled branches testified to better days.

Soon it was time to move on again.

The plant centre cautioned me about digging it up in the wrong season. I decided to take the risk and chopped it back, wrenched it from the ground, and put it in a pot.

Every day I watched and watered it. For a couple of weeks, it just sat there but it didn't die. Then one day I noticed a couple of leaves and knew that my rose—and I—would survive.

I picked the bush's first rose and lovingly placed it in a vase, thanking God for this reminder that He'd turned up yet again.

Gradually I learned to hold both joy and sadness at once, instead of allowing sorrow to elbow its way into full occupancy and make life miserable.

A good counsellor showed me the way to re-story this chapter of my journey and fit it in—scars, warts and all.

As I healed, I saw again that...

The Sun Will Come Up Tomorrow

I've been walking the beach in the mornings, enjoying the summer weather and hopefully benefiting from the wonderful sea air.

I love the constancy of the waves. On windless days they ripple onto the shore; in the storms, they crash and roar as they hit the sand—and they just keep coming.

Each day the sun rises a little later over Rangitoto Island. Interestingly, it comes up in a slightly different place every morning.

Today was spectacular. The huge golden ball of light erupted from the very top of the volcanic cone and burst into huge shafts, spilling down onto the sea. It was a perfect morning and I confess to feeling quite inspired by the sheer majesty of it all.

There have many times, however, when I walked the beach on a grey, rainy day and hardly noticed the sunrise at all; times when things were so tough that I wondered what tomorrow may bring. I 'couldn't see the wood for the trees' or in this case, I couldn't see the sun for the mountain. But like Little Orphan

Annie, I eventually accepted that the sun will rise again tomorrow.

It's that constancy again—in a world full of unpredictability, there are some things that keep on keeping on.

I don't know about you, but I find that so comforting.

It's an interesting observation that when my life falls awry, the earth does not fall off its axis in sympathy. I'm learning to trust in a bigger plan.

Solving Life

During long winter nights, I like to have a jigsaw puzzle on the go. I light the fire and set out the pieces on the coffee table and slowly but surely it comes together.

Other people are more methodical and do all the borders first, but I tend to go for instant gratification and end up with little bits all over the place. But one way or another I eventually get the big picture.

My puzzle-puddling gives me time to philosophize about life. If I believe I've been intelligently designed with a wonderful big picture in mind, it's so much easier not to worry when I can't see where all the pieces fit. If I'm part of a master plan, I can go back again and again and look at the picture on the box to see how it's supposed to look when it's finished.

Unlike my jigsaw puzzle I probably won't be able to witness the complete picture of my life this side of puzzle heaven, but one thing my puzzles and I share. At the very end we both get carried out in a box.

Oops! did I just say that?

Before I rush off to choose my coffin, I have more lessons to learn and more to share…

Pick Your Battles

I could call this episode "Confessions of a Divorce Recovery Facilitator". It sounds clumsy, but I learned some things in this role.

One year a woman attended my seminar because her husband had had a better offer and ran off with a younger woman. She was understandably devastated. Fast forward two years and the younger woman came through the course, too.

"Why did he leave me for another woman?" she sobbed. "He said he would never leave me. He said his first wife was impossible and that my love made him whole. He said I completed him." (Cue—soundtrack from *Jerry Maguire*.)

I met people determined to hold on to bitterness and resentment because somehow it fuelled their lives.

Some stories shocked me; including that of the man whose wife had placed false child sexual abuse charges against him. He spent all his money in his defence and by the time he attended the course he still had no access to his children.

Many women there presumed that dead-beat dad would turn into 'Father of the Year' after the separation, and would turn up for every visit on time, bearing gifts. The 'Disneyland' parent who lived in luxury would bring lots of presents, and was so much more fun than the real, custodial parent who took on the grinding, everyday responsibilities.

Many separation agreements stalled over the smallest of

conditions. One lawyer referred to her "knife and fork" cases, in which divorcing couples spent thousands of dollars fighting over who got the cutlery. The applicant needs the money more than the lawyer does, and wisdom informs that a flash canteen of cutlery is no substitute for peace.

Note to self... always arrange a pre-nuptial agreement, even if, in your loved-up state, you don't think you need one. Remember that this romantic feeling is a bit like madness and can lead to a commitment which comes back and haunts you.

If your marriage fails, take responsibility for your part in the break-up. Then move on.

I've realised that, sometimes, horrible people stay married due to the imminent canonization of one of the spouses; being single does not make you a lesser saint.

If you find the perfect mate, don't marry them... they deteriorate very quickly.

There's a tendency when you fall in love to think you would give everything for the object of your affection.

Unconditional love can be a bit tricky.

Don't offer people the world, then deliver the Atacama Desert. That's a dry-as-a-bone recipe for disaster. I now put boundaries on my affections.

Thank goodness my training as a facilitator taught me that a dad's role in a child's life is vital. Unless there's a history of abuse, contact should be maintained as much as possible. You do your children a great disservice by slagging off their father and it leads to huge problems down the track. To this day my children enjoy a good relationship with their dad.

Daddy's Girl

There's been a lot in the media about boys and men in our society. It seems that boys have lagged behind educationally and there's concern about the effect that fatherlessness is having on them. Dads are so important for both boys and girls.

A dad called a parenting talk-back recently and I thought what he said was really neat. He'd realized that he couldn't address all the ills of young people and he was worried that his daughter was growing up in a scary adolescent world. At first, he felt powerless to protect her, but he couldn't keep her at home forever. So, he decided that he would build into her some defences that she could use herself.

As she reached puberty, he began to treat her like a young lady. He opened the car door for her, took her on an occasional date and generally taught her to be treated with respect by a man. He also made sure he treated her mother really well.

He understood that, increasingly, she would have to stand alone and make tough choices. But at least he felt he was doing something positive, and that her future suitors would have a hard act to follow.

There you are, dads... you have a lot more power than you probably realise. Set the standard high and one day your little girl will thank you for it.

Dad's Rule!

On the day before Mother's Day, I sat in a jewellery shop waiting for a watch to be repaired. Now, I'm not one to sit patiently but they had free coffee on tap and the shop was beautiful, showcasing shining diamonds and bling. The air was electric with love and romance. Couples held hands while gazing into trays of engagement rings. People wandered in, wondering if something special would turn up under their pillow the next day.

One little girl in particular caught my eye. About eight or nine, she was on a mission. Clutched in her hand was a long list written with a large, black felt pen of possibilities for her Mum's day. I glimpsed plants, clothes and earrings. To be sure it would be the right choice, she'd brought Dad along. She was dressed for the occasion—a cute, pink princess top with matching floral jeans and sparkling slip-on shoes. It was patently clear that dad was the accessory, the handbag—or in this case, the wallet—in her shopping expedition.

It was so sweet to watch him. He dutifully followed her around the shop, discussing the options and sharing her enthusiasm. He gently steered her away from the items that would blow the budget.

There's nothing more inspiring than a dad spending time with his daughter and honouring her mother at the same time.

33

Olden Days

The question on my mind after recovering from my latest relationship debacle was. "What next"?

At that stage, I juggled three part-time jobs and the onset of my senior years. I had to slow down or end up in the parallel universe I've dubbed the 'dementia-graphic'.

The first step was to buy a new car.

Fries with That?

I ventured into the dodgy world of the car salesman. I discovered that new cars come with only the rudiments of vehicle necessities and anything else costs mega-bucks more. Evidently, it's called 'upspecing', a bit like upsizing your coke at McDonalds.

I could have a better, flasher steering wheel, airbags that pop out from every direction, brakes that could stop a ten-tonne truck, and wheels in mag, alloy or—if I was very cheap—humble steel. The salesman looked really depressed at the prospect of steel wheels. They are so 'yesterday' and reek with the stench of reduced commissions.

Poor guy, he sold his little heart out and came up trumpless. The cars he offered were all too expensive. I went home and trawled through the Saturday paper with the idea of taking a trip instead.

In travel advertising, most hidden taxes, fuel surcharges, and government fees are hidden in the fine print. The real clincher is that most 'reasonable' fares are advertised 'one way'. How on earth was I supposed to get home?

Maybe they get you there and then double the return fare?

That's exactly what happens. When you realise you could end up pan-handling in Peru, you become highly motivated to buy—in advance—the fare home.

It was all too hard, so I went to McDonalds for lunch. The waiter asked, "Would you like fries with that and would you like them upsized?" The look I gave him would've cut through a stack of Big Macs.

It was time to set some new...

Priorities

I've never been a perfectionist and probably settle too often for mediocrity. The pursuit of perfection doesn't look like much fun to me and is very hard work. Although I concentrate and reign my brain in, I think weird and totally unacceptable things at times.

I'm greatly encouraged by Anne Lamott who said that "perfectionism is the voice of the oppressor" and "I thought such awful thoughts, I cannot even say them out loud because they would make Jesus want to drink gin straight out of the cat dish."

I've fallen off almost every wagon that would consent to carry me, including the chocolate wagon, the wine wagon, and the diet wagon.

Dieting is a biggy. I'm capable of noble aspirations one minute while finding myself like a large horse with its nose buried in a nosebag the next, neighing my way to nutritional nirvana.

I instinctively know that I'll die one day – clever eh? As Erma Bombeck observed, we should "Seize the moment... remembering all those women on the Titanic who waved off the dessert cart".

Would it be unkind to suggest they survived because someone was able to hoist them into a lifeboat?

I don't want to upset the apple-pie cart and I do try to find a life balance but it's not always easy back in the real world.

Busy, Busy

My daughter, Tracey, feels overwhelmed by all the things she's signed up for. She sent me this piece about how she's handling it.

"We're busy people. In fact, I think we might be busier than you. My husband and I both work full-time. He's in charge of music at our local church, and we own a recording studio. Did I mention we moved into a new house less than a year ago?

"And I admit I find some comfort in being busy. There can be a feeling of importance because so many people want my time. But I've noticed my priorities are a little skewed of late, and my kids suffer the fall-out of overwork.

"They're more emotional and more demanding. My husband and I bicker and feel removed from our friends. We need a break! Easier said than done, I know, but even God rested on the seventh day.

"I wished for a short, concise way to opt out of a few things. In a weak moment, I paused to draw breath, and had a mini epiphany. There's a perfect word in the English language and that word is, 'No'.

"My goal over the next few months is to use it. But I plan to say 'yes' more to my kids and my husband and to create some time for me."

She's a wise girl, Tracey. I think I'll listen to her.

Going 'hell-bent for leather' may have worked well for cowboys or the pony express but there are other ways to live...

Stuff and Nonsense

I've had the privilege of traveling to South America, following the ancient paths of the Inca people, tracing their bloody history of devastation at the hands of the Spanish Conquistadores. Their oppressors stripped them of most of their gold, carting it back to an impoverished Spain. The Incans were amazed at the Conquistadores' insatiable need for gold. At the beginning they thought the Spaniards must eat it and, in some bizarre way, it helped to ward off sickness.

Some of it made its way into the ornate cathedrals which seem almost grotesque in these poor countries.

I met many descendants of these ancient people and I suspect they have a better appreciation for what's important than I do.

Those living away from the cities still plough with oxen, live in mud-brick houses, and live off the land. They all practice a hybrid religion—a mixture of Catholic and Incan faiths tailor-made for their survival.

One thing is certain, they are a spiritual people who reject the pull of materialism in favour of a simple life. They make sure they have plenty of time for each other. The natural balance of their everyday living shows they value the spiritual life above material things.

The trip certainly challenged me to re-examine my priorities and to make sure the people I love receive more attention than the possessions I own. Using things but loving people is a good way to live.

Fame, fortune and a perfect body? These have eluded me and yet I become more contented every day.

Charles Spurgeon said, "It is beyond the realm of possibilities that one has the ability to out-give God. Even if I give the whole of my worth to Him, He will find a way to give back much more than I gave'." Perhaps by giving away we find life to the full.

Cross Purposes

While I watched the Oscars recently – the epitome of public recognition, the pinnacle of fame and success – the line-up of talented and gorgeous actors was impressive, and the audience applauded and praised. The winners exhorted us all to excellence, world peace, tolerance and humility. This glittering occasion would be the closest thing—barring a game between the All Blacks and the Wallabies—to hero worship.

Over 2000 years ago, another man stepped on to the world stage and spoke of hope and a new start for all of us. He said there was a way to joy and peace and immortality. He said that if we believed him, we could rise above our circumstances and taste heaven on earth. He said he believed it so much he'd get it for us even if it killed him.

No-one nominated Jesus for an Oscar; he received no fancy tuxedo, no champagne, no limo, only a couple of thieves as his supporting cast in the final scene of his drama; just ridicule, a loincloth, some vinegar, and his own beaten body to carry him to glory. Even Tinseltown could never adequately portray the impact of his death on a crude cross.

In Hollywood, it seems to me a man can relatively easily become a god, but I know of only one God who was prepared to become a man.

I think, with the spiritual hole in mankind's heart he can never be satisfied by stuff and nonsense. Yet we build our paltry kingdoms, acquire our empty baubles, and find more idols to worship. It seems to me we can't live without worshipping something. The question is, will the objects of our highest time and resource-consuming efforts ever bring lasting happiness? Yet we keep trying, salving our souls with sips of the latest wines, shoes, houses and holidays. We talk about them, compare them to other people's, and briefly bask in the sun of our superiority until something better titillates our taste buds and we're back on the yellow-brick road to the next best thing.

Even religions are not immune to their sacred cows, as their leaders strut, dripping in fine clothes and jewellery, paying lip service to the poor and needy.

I understand why Jesus's presence upset the religious leaders of the time. They expected the prophesied future king to be a powerful man on a white horse cutting a swathe through their enemies and expecting to be elevated to where they belonged. Instead He talked about laying down your life for others, giving all your goods to the poor, turning the other cheek and other stuff that wasn't too popular. He came to earth largely unannounced.

He arrived...

Undercover

I sometimes find basic Christian beliefs a bit bewildering. The idea that anyone would want to step out of a world of wealth and privilege and live among the poor, the distressed, and the hopeless seems unlikely to me.

But then I watched *Undercover Boss* on TV and it struck me that this is a good example of what God did. He sent the CEO of his firm to live on earth and to experience all the challenges and stresses of ordinary folk like us. In Jesus's case, he waited thirty years before he told everybody who he really was. The difference—once people heard the message that he'd come from God to save them, most of them decided that they'd like to get rid of him.

Now the TV program and faith part company. Can you imagine the recipients on the Undercover Boss show telling the CEO to stick his generosity and get lost?

But many, if not all, of Jesus' friends deserted him.

Maybe God's offer was not quite so palatable. He said we could have love, joy and peace but these come with developing longsuffering, patience, and tolerance. Perhaps He should have offered free university scholarships, new cars, instant finance and a lifetime supply of dog food.

34

Money Matters

Epicurus wrote, "Nothing is enough for the man to whom enough is too little".

An unhealthy nagging in our souls to chase material things leads us to think the next purchase will seal the deal of contentment. It's like putting your life in a bucket full of holes.

'More' compels, and especially 'quick more'.

> **Money that comes easily disappears quickly,**
> **but money that is gathered little by little will grow.**
>
> *Proverbs 13*

Many people have commented that, despite my financial setbacks, I'm in a financially secure place in my semi-retirement. I put the emphasis on semi because I don't believe an entrepreneur ever retires.

I've learned a few lessons which I plan to inflict on you right now!

I moaned about money—or the lack of it—one day, having unexpected big bills, and feeling stressed. Then I read that, as average Kiwis, we live a lifestyle in the top 10% of people in the world. A huge percentage of people on our planet don't have enough food or a roof over their heads. They don't have clean water or access to education or reasonable health care which certainly brings our financial wants and needs into perspective.

I read some money wisdom that went like this:

"Money will never satisfy our spiritual needs. It can buy a bed but not a peaceful sleep; it can buy a house but not a home. It can buy food but not an appetite; it can buy diamonds but not love."

It's a hard lesson to learn, that money doesn't buy happiness. I have no desire to return to the financial struggles of my past, but I see that I spend far too much time thinking and talking about money. In the end, money won't get me into heaven, and it won't save foundering relationships, or stop me dying eventually.

Faith, hope and love are the best investments I can make for my future.

Money may talk, it may even shout, but in the end, you have a choice—you either love it or use it.

Light My Fire

I'm not a winter person. I feel the need to curl into a ball and hibernate for the few months until daffodils daff and spring lambs spring before I stick my nose out the window like a groundhog and sniff the air for signs of summer. It seems like for weeks I've been chasing polar bears off the front lawn and powering through the firewood.

I've spent a lot of time coaxing my fireplace into action. I think there are lessons to be learned pertaining to 'home and hearth' and what builds a solid, enduring, warm family.

Firstly, you need matches—something to capture the family's attention. Maybe some simple ideas like hugs and little notes. Then you need kindling wood—small random acts of kindness to carry warmth to the bigger issues and deeper intimacies. It must be built right, as I've discovered. You can't dump the big bits on top and hope they'll catch fire. If they're too big they smother the flames and you must start again.

Sometimes, in my impatience, I've poked around too much instead of letting the kindling flame grow big enough to do the job. I've found, especially with teenagers, that backing off is more effective than using volatile accelerants like accusations and angry words. Sometimes flaming family situations need time to cool before taking action.

It's OK if it doesn't work the first time. I messed up and bungled my way through parenting on many occasions and needed to start again on really important issues.

Like fire-lighting, I've found that if you keep trying, you will succeed with glowing logs and warm hearts in your family.

I am indomitably opportunistic, constantly seeking solutions to any life problems that rear their ugly heads. This attitude results in people pouring out their hearts to me. Some are total strangers. They ask my advice and boy do they get it! My friends have dubbed this "The Frances Talk". This brings me to my ...

Encounters

I believe that you never know if a stranger is an angel in disguise, so I talk to anyone short of Attila the Hun. Such encounters happen in cafés, on the beach, in meetings, on planes, in airports and in foreign countries.

I sat on the beach one day after a romp in the surf, when a drop-dead gorgeous man plopped next to me. After some chit-chat, he bared his soul about his broken marriage, his children's reaction, and his worries about the future. I gave him some advice, reassured him that as an involved dad he was doing his best. After thirty minutes he thanked me and left.

One day in a crowded café, a woman asked if she could share my table and proceeded to tell me her life story. She brought her daughter to see me the following week for a talk.

Sometimes these encounters happen when I'm at a real low point in my own heart.

Alone at a table for two, I had a coffee when the waitress asked if she could steal my extra chair for a group coming to a table next door. It had been a lonely week for me and the last thing I needed was to be reminded that I was 'Nigel-no-mates', but I bit my tongue and gave up the extra chair. A man sat at the table next to me and the waitress asked him if he, too, could move to make space for the group, so he asked me if he could sit at my table. I said he'd have to find a chair. A pleasant-enough hour ensued with chit-chat, mainly about him and his sand-sifting job which wasn't entirely riveting.

Next thing, the group arrived, and one man there leaned over and asked if he could have the sugar tray at my table. That's when I lost it.

"No, you cannot", I said, "You've taken my chair and lumped me with this bloke and now you want my sugar as well?"

Poor guy looked a bit scared, so I laughed and let him in on the joke. I find you can get away with a lot if your mouth is turned up at the corners!

Meanwhile Mr Sand-sifter asked if I'd like to go to the movies with him which I didn't. I saw him again a few months later with what looked like a real girlfriend.

Another beach meeting occurred as I wobbled along on a stick after surgery, when a handsome young man of Indian descent asked me if I lived here and commented on what a paradise it was. We got chatting. He told me he was an international engineer. He tried to convert me to his form of Buddhism. He grasped my hand and told me love was the answer to all of life's ills.

Then he offered to vacuum my house. I have concluded that he was a vacuum cleaner salesman.

Which, at a stretch, could be considered an international engineer.

Operation Stupidity

I blame it on the surgery which left me house-bound for a couple of months. The grinding loneliness which had catapulted me into a disastrous marriage returned with a vengeance.

This time, I told myself, I was older and wiser and would treat the whole process like a job interview or an application for life insurance.

So, I decided to put myself back on the "meet" market and signed up to an online dating site.

First up was an attractive, articulate man who seemed a likely candidate but was rather resistant to my interview style, sliding out from underneath most of the questions with alarming alacrity. However, he seemed rather physically responsive, almost sitting in my lap after about thirty minutes. He walked me to my car and effused about how wonderful I was and that he would love to see me again. I have no idea what he found so compelling because he knew very little about me. Twenty minutes later I got a message through the site that told me he just wasn't that into me. I think he was looking more for Ms Right-now than Ms Right. Luckily it took more than that for me to fall in love, so I scraped him off and moved on.

Another candidate suggested we should try lying in bed all day and making love over and over and doing lots of giggling. I couldn't imagine anything more boring and as he was quite elderly, I think he was a bit optimistic about his performance abilities.

Next was a nice bloke who lived in assisted housing because he lost all his money in business. I decided being an ace Scrabble player would not form the basis for an ongoing relationship.

My search continues...

I put the search for Mr Wonderful on hold while I galloped to celebrate my seventieth birthday in a villa in Tuscany, as you do.

First things first, I consulted my surgeon who, a few months before the trip, had attempted to retrieve vestiges of tendons in my left hip, clamp them onto anything that still existed and get me back on my feet.

Evidently seventeen years of scaling Machu Picchu, a few years of ballroom dancing, combined with an excessive number of steroid shots to keep me mobile, had finally taken their toll. The shots had not made me into Ms Universe, and it would appear I had peaked too early for the next Olympics, so surgery was my last resort.

The big question was, could I recover in time for my big trip?

Hip, Hip, X-ray

Other people, people with wisdom and maturity, organise a significant birthday party at a restaurant or have some special friends around for a dinner with cake.

But not me! I hatched a plan to travel to Italy. I mooted the idea to a few people and twenty-eight expressed interest.

"Don't worry about a thing," I enthused, "I'll organise the itinerary, book all the guides and hotels and excursions. You just have to cough up a few thousand and we're good to go".

It took a year in the planning. Every detail was researched and scrutinized. Poor old Trip Advisor was flogged to death.

Finally, the guest number whittled down to nine. All were friends whom I'd known for over fifty years, including my brother, whom, surprisingly, I'd known all his life. He's a doctor so at least I knew he would look after me if said tendons disappeared into the ether.

Old Friends

First, we had a practice run, and went away for a weekend together. We rented a house beside a lake and spent the weekend having fun, reminiscing, and solving the world's problems.

Collectively we share over 400 years of friendship and about 350 years of marriage, though we all think we look really young.

Our conversation was a veritable feast ranging from politics to parenting to faith.

We discussed personality types, nature over nurture in raising children, and our hopes for our future grandchildren.

And we laughed—at ourselves, at the absurdity of life, at some of our younger days when we were so idealistic. We compared middle-aged spreads (I won that one hands down) and we ate tons of healthy food, knowing that 'the diet starts after the weekend', or not!

We tramped around the lake, watched old movies, and put up with one bathroom. Nobody grumped or moaned or snapped.

None of this seems remarkable, unless you know we are all very different people. Our jobs range from a university lecturer to businessmen. The common denominator, I've worked out, is that we truly love each another and over the years we've celebrated our respective journeys. We've stood by each other through thick and thicker and sometimes agreed to disagree.

So, here's to old friendships. They're worth their weight in gold.

I rounded up some usual suspects, added another couple to the mix and off we went.

Stylish in Venice

Some of us had met earlier, in Venice, where our hotel provided an enchanting roof terrace. We sat and sipped a rich red, pinching ourselves while gazing across centuries of stunning architecture in this sinking city. That first night, after leaning out my window and listening to music from the canal below, I left my shutters ajar and fell into heavy-lidded, jet-lagged slumber, water lapping against the piles and gondolas creaking gently against their moorings.

The houses in Venice seem slightly tipsy, as if they've imbibed too much wine. They tilt and teeter over their watery habitats like ancient, giant Lego structures. It's understandable when you learn they're built on millions of petrified logs hauled from the Dolomites and hammered into the salty marshes below. Many houses are now habitable only from the second floor up, as waters of the lagoon gradually eat away at the foundations.

There is nothing quite as inspiring as listening to Vivaldi's

Four Seasons played by a top-class baroque orchestra, in an ancient church, followed by a night stroll alongside the canal, over which hangs a full moon spilling its beams on to the city below.

I'd been to Venice once before in the company of a less than agreeable companion, so this visit was redemptive, and I saturated myself in the sheer joy of even the kitschy bits.

At our final dinner we were serenaded by gondoliers gliding by the restaurant singing their tenor hearts out. One thing that hits you *in the eye like a big pizza pie* in Italy is their amazing commitment to looking good. Design is everywhere, especially in the clothes. Men are not afraid to strut their stuff in vibrant colours, and snazzy loafers sans socks. Even the vaporetto driver wore an exquisite linen shirt with a cool cashmere sweater casually draped over his shoulders—not to mention the designer sunglasses and coiffed hairdo.

One guide said, waving his hands around with enthusiasm, "We're Italian, which means things may not work, but they look good and are fun." I couldn't agree more. His eyebrows were appropriately plucked.

In his book, *The Italians,* John Hooper expands on the culture.

"Scepticism about ever being able to reach firm conclusions is both reflected in, and encouraged by, the Italian language. The word *verita* means truth. But it also means version. If a dispute arises, there will be my *verita*, your *verita* and doubtless the various *verita* of others.

Much the same approach can be discerned in the reluctance of the Italian media to provide readers with the facts they need to make judgements on what is said by public figures."

Philosophising about the political system is not nearly as much fun as celebrating their unabashed commitment to having a good time. Who am I to argue with that? The best plan is to revel in it and go for broke.

Given the absence of motor vehicles, everything is delivered by boat including large appliances and building materials.

Truth or not, religious relics have generated millions of visitors and probably billions of dollars over the years. That's if you can stand the crowds in St Mark's Square and the shuffle through the Basilica.

According to Wikipedia, "...in 828, relics believed to be the body of Saint Mark were stolen from Alexandria (at the time controlled by the Abbasid Caliphate) by two Venetian merchants with the help of two Greek monks, and taken to Venice. A mosaic in St Mark's Basilica depicts sailors covering the relics with a layer of pork and cabbage leaves. Since Muslims are not permitted to touch pork, this was done to prevent the guards from inspecting the ship's cargo too closely. In 1063, during the construction of a new basilica in Venice, Saint Mark's relics could not be found. However, according to tradition, in 1094, the Saint himself revealed the location of his remains by extending an arm from a pillar. The new-found remains were placed in a sarcophagus in the basilica."

This gives new meaning to the words—'a hand-out'.

Although all but sixty thousand people have abandoned the city due to increasing costs, it remains an artistic, architectural, and spiritual testament to an enterprising, paranoid, exotic and erotic culture. Every alley, canal, and beauteous building tells and hides tales. It's mind-boggling that a small diaspora of beleaguered people could have created this marvel and morphed it into this opulent and unashamed display of excess.

With *O Sole Mio* and *Volare* still ringing in our eras, a smooth, almost soundless train rocked us to Florence where Massimo was waiting to transport us out of the city. We left behind the crowds and slowly the tar-sealed roads dwindled into narrow, gravelled lanes.

I tell you, you haven't lived until you've spent five nights in an 18th century villa south of Florence with your besties-for-life. Perched on the hillside, our villa peers over the valley. Wisteria drapes from the pergolas like long eyelashes framing the vistas below.

The Prosecco tanker backed up to the front door, the food arrived miraculously from somewhere, and we spent our days roaming the rolling Tuscany countryside, amongst the vineyards and the poppies. The views from our lofty bedrooms were stunning, with iconic soldier-like cypress trees and classic stone, terracotta-roofed houses in the distance. I threw open the shutters of my exquisitely decorated digs, complete with bright yellow-tiled en suite, and bit into the visual feast from my room-with-a-view.

Someone produced music from their phone and, with the combined memories of mostly senior citizens, we managed to belt out many of the songs of the 50s to the 70s. The dancing was to die for—seriously, it nearly killed us.

But mainly we cared for each other, sharing our deepest secrets, failures and successes and getting to know each other like never before. It was nothing short of special and everything I hoped for.

Bathed in the scenic beauty of Tuscany, we explored our neighbourhood. We dipped into Castellina Chianti, sampling the local wine and food and finding out about the Etruscans. They were a matriarchal society before it was the 'in thing', even building their tombs in the shape of pregnant bellies complete with navels. I'm not sure where my navel is these days but, thanking God that I will never be "with child" again, I moved on to wine tasting.

After the villa, we took the train to Naples then transferred via Pompeii.

One wonders if the citizens of Pompeii had any warning before the eruption. Quora tells me, "They had lived with the volcano forever, and for the most part it was a genial if grumpy neighbour. They had recovered from a significant earthquake a few years before and many no doubt assumed that it wouldn't be that bad".

The petrified remains of humans and animals testifies that it was 'that bad'—and rather macabre; but the remains of the city tell a story of incredible engineering sophistication. Underfloor heating and saunas were commonplace in their homes. If you needed a brothel, an undeniable emblem had been blazoned into the street pointing in the right direction.

After touring the ruins, our driver negotiated the precipitous narrow roads to deposit us safely at our hotel on the Amalfi Coast. Our Positano hotel was poised high above the town, clinging to the cliffs by its toenails. We could reach it by climbing over four hundred steps or taking a small bus that ground up and down the hairpin-bend roads all day long.

We stayed six nights and gradually explored the nooks and

crannies of this delightful place, finding surprising restaurants cantilevered over the outcrops and cute boutiques dotted down the hillsides.

This was where I poured out my appreciation to my surgeon. With the help of the group, we all managed to complete the Walk of the Gods, a pretty challenging seven kilometres along a precipitous path high in the hills. At one stage I was literally pushed up a gravelly bank. Hysterical laughter from me didn't help, but the hiking pole did the trick and I celebrated with a limoncello. Cattle prod anyone?

Napoleon tried to turn Capri into another Gibraltar but was eventually knocked off this perch by the French and the island was reclaimed by the Bourbons of Naples. Getting there took fifty minutes of sheer joy, boating across the turquoise water on the fast ferry.

Getting up Mount Solero was a bit fraught as I still required my stick, and my efforts to mount the chairlift must have been a sight to behold as I was whacked in the backside by the chair scooping me up. Suspended at about six hundred metres above sea level is a bit of a shock, but the soundless ride gives you time to listen to birdsong and scan the houses and gardens below. We stood spellbound on the top and gazed across the Tyrrhenian Sea thanking God for the beauty of creation.

Rome was not built in a day, and we spent several days wandering around imbibing the Caesars and the Popes. I feel uncomfortable with the wealth of the Vatican and wonder how Jesus's simple message of sharing and suffering translated into opulence and privilege. Yet the art is beautiful and reflects the best of mankind's soul.

I loved the Mum-and-Pop small restaurants, most offering hearty Italian fare. I have to say though, that a good flat white is still best in New Zealand.

One dude whose name pops up a lot in the annuls of the Roman Empire is Hadrian. Born near Seville, he built massive villas around town. He also built a wall in the north of England and constructed arches in Jordan, Athens and Turkey.

As Mary Beard says, "His most famous building in Rome was the great Pantheon. One of the few ancient Roman buildings to remain standing at its full height, and even now in active use as a church, it is crowned with what is still the largest dome ever built with unreinforced concrete. It has been impossible to see Nero as anything other than a rapacious megalomaniac, but Hadrian has morphed conveniently into cultured art collector and amateur architect. Where Nero's relationships with men have to be seen as part of the corruption of his reign, Hadrian has been turned into a troubled gay. Hadrian seems familiar to us—for we have made him so."

In 130 AD he travelled to Jerusalem and rebuilt the city according to his own designs and renamed it after himself and a Roman god. As you can imagine, that went down like a ton of bricks and when the Jews rebelled, he mercilessly slaughtered almost 600,000 of them.

He established cities throughout the Balkan Peninsula, Egypt, Asia Minor, and Greece. At one stage to tried to make Athens the capital of the empire. It shows that genius and megalomania can go hand in hand. Myth or truth? Who knows?

In Greece

In Greece I accessed my inner Zorba and ate and drank and danced my way across this ancient land. It's hard for an Antipodean with such recent history to take on board such antiquity. I viewed artefacts that are eight thousand years old and a mechanism said to be the world's oldest computer from about 100 BC. I also stood at the spot in Corinth where St Paul was tried and found innocent.

Historically they're a beaten-up people, the Greeks, and it's reflected in their sometimes-melancholic music. Yet their joy is revealed in exuberant, colourful dance and their zest for life. At least somebody is making a fortune out of the manufacture of breakable plates for us gullible tourists. The dire financial straits of the nation appear as a sub-text. They're used to hard times but celebrating the present is essential, as is a compelling life philosophy.

A visit to the monasteries at Meteora and our guide's explanation of the geological formations in the area, prompted some thoughts.

Here were monks dedicated to their faith and prepared to go the extra miles to live it except their miles were up vertical rocks.

In 1350, an ascetic monk named Varlaam climbed one great rock and settled at the top. He built three churches, a cell for himself and a water tank. No one chose to follow his lead, so after his death the site was abandoned.

The buildings fell into ruin for almost two hundred years until 1517, when two rich priest-monks, Theophanes and Nektarios Apsarades from Ioanina, ascended the rock and founded a monastery. According to legend, they had to drive away the monster who lived in a cave on the summit before they could move in.

The brothers renovated Varlaam's Church of the Three Hierarchs, erected the tower, and built a katholikon (1541-42) dedicated to All Saints. Using ropes, pulleys and baskets, it took twenty-two years to hoist all the building materials to the top of the rock. Once everything was at the top, the construction work took only twenty days.

One person asked how often they replaced the ropes on the pulleys to which the monk wryly smiled and said, "Only when they break".

During WWII, Meteora was bombed and many of the treasures were looted.

The makeup of the rock fascinated me. It's called 'conglomerate', a combination of thousands of years of natural products forced together by earth, wind, fire and water, one upheaval after another. If you look closely you'll even see seashells.

In Contemplation

Most of the important things in life I've learned from pressure and hard times, not from dining on bowls of cherries. In hindsight I'm grateful for all of them. Tough times are like compost to a plant. They cause us to dig deep, they build character when personality is not enough to get us through. Hardship makes us question our own rightness, our own entitlement to all things instant and accessible.

T. S. Eliot said,

"...the end of all our exploring

Will be to arrive where we started
And know the place for the first time".

We may have to go around the mountain a few times to get back to where we belong.

Don't get me wrong, I crave an easy life, but I'd rather be remembered for how I coped under duress than how I blossomed in success.

I sat looking into the valley below and thought about the monks inching their way to the top, one rung at a time. It occurred to me that I'm able to practice my faith partly because they were prepared to defend theirs against all odds.

I poked around the back streets of Athens, drinking in the local vibe. My three-score-years-and-ten anniversary triggered introspection on what the rest of my life could look like.

I ordered a frappe at a funny little street café. I must have seemed to be an oddity in this off-the-beaten-tourist-track, as several older Greek men sat and stared at me the whole time I was there.

A lone ranger must also take risks—missing buses, trains and flights; or getting lost and relying on the kindness of strangers. Her resources are challenging, and her fears are confronting, but rung by rung she claws her way to confidence and a growing sense that she is part of a bigger picture.

According to Greek myth, the first god to exist was Chaos or 'the Void' and everything came forth from there. My wanderings helped me make sense of this Chaotic city, which seems to hang together somehow. The word 'catharsis' is also Greek and maybe that too is part of my journey.

I'm not too comfortable with this solo wandering thing but, as I abandon time and plans, I begin to understand the value of pointless meandering. I've read that a bit of ennui is good for us anyway. This from The Guardian...

"Far from dulling the mind and leading to a lack of productivity, boredom can inspire people to seek out ways of being altruistic, empathetic, and to engage in pro-social tasks, particularly the unpleasant ones such as giving blood."

Thankfully no blood was needed at that time, so I trotted back to my hotel to rest up before the long flights home to New Zealand.

* * *

My seventy years has not been lived in isolation. I'm the "conglomeration" of countless people who taught me everything I know and fought, even in recent history, for the freedoms I enjoy. Even this book is a rich series of plagiarisms from the authors who have ripped my heart to shreds with their brilliant insights into the human condition and made me laugh raucously at their wry words. I've been to places I'd never set foot in, 'where angels fear to tread'; I've found solutions for problems that've reared their ugly heads and yelled for me to quit.

Anne Lamott says, "Being a writer gives you an excuse to go places and explore. Another is that writing causes us to look closely at life as it lurches by and tramps around".

I've never been able to live a life of pretence. I can't skim over the top or walk through without touching the edges. I'm constantly absorbing and observing situations and behaviours and filtering them through my own experience. Sometimes it's a burden. I want to slough off my insight or go away with the fairies. I want to be 'footloose and fancy free' and not give a hoot about you, or me, or the local lamppost with a bulb which has blown. I don't want to see when you or I are getting it wrong and stuffing up our lives.

My body has an extreme reaction to excess alcohol so I can't even pass into a drug-induced oblivion. Deep sleep is my only refuge. As soon as a new day dawns, my eyes flutter like shutters on a camera and I begin my panoramic scope of life with eyes wide open.

36

Optical Illusions

In Portugal, Spain, and the French Riviera, the cost of beach-side properties is very high, and the cost of an apartment with a balcony is even pricier. Enterprising artists earn their living painting false balconies—complete with flower boxes and even washing lines pegged with lacy smalls—on the walls of houses. These murals are known as tromp l'oeil or 'trick of the eye', so realistic, it's hard to tell that they're not the real thing until you get up close.

In Roman times, large, clay water pots were bought and sold in the markets. Sometimes, if a pot cracked, crooked tradesmen would patch them with wax and then try to sell them as new and undamaged. Honest vendors put signs on their pots, guaranteeing that they were sin cere, Latin for 'without wax'. In English this word is 'sincere'.

In Greek drama, actors wore masks so they could play male and female parts and the audience wouldn't know the difference.

"All the world's a stage" said Shakespeare, "and we are merely players."

I know I play many parts: wife, mother, friend, employee and caregiver. And the real me often doesn't show unless someone gets really close. That's when I feel most authentic, when I let it all hang out—warts, dirty laundry, the whole shebang.

So, this is a tribute to all those who let me be me. Your patience and tolerance have not gone unnoticed.

Meanwhile, my knapsack is on my back again and I'm off for more lessons.

On a trip to Spain, I commented to our tour guide that she didn't say very much about Christopher Columbus.

"Well," she said, "we have a joke we tell here, and it goes like this...

"When Christopher Columbus left Spain, he didn't know where he was going. When he got there, he didn't know where he was. And when he returned, he didn't know where he'd been."

This set me thinking about how we change our lives, how we go in different directions and hopefully end up in better places. For me, the first thing I had to do was to decide honestly where I was at the moment.

Imagine, if I called a travel agent and said I wanted to go to Queenstown; what if her first question is, "Where are you now?" and I say, "I have no idea." Where was I and where did I want to go?

I decided to let it be for a moment and just wander.

When travelling, you can't help but notice that 'peace on earth and goodwill towards man' is not exactly driving the world. Through the ages, it never seemed to matter what political persuasion ruled a country; greed and self-actualization reared their ugly heads all over the place. Being selfless and kind are difficult attitudes to legislate.

If only the powers-that-be would listen to Winnie the Pooh...

37

Pooh Parable

To bring about world peace, all we need is to ensure the entire earth's population watches Winnie the Pooh's Heffalump movie. Amelia watched it with me. My first lesson was to come prepared with food. 'Cos it's hard to sit still for a long time without food, and sharing food is a good way to get along better with the people you're with.

In the movie, Pooh and his friends decide on an expedition to capture Heffalumps, huge trumpeting creatures that lived in Heffalump Hollow. Pooh and Co were scared stiff of them, so they carried all sorts of home-grown weapons.

Little Roo was too small to be in the posse, but curiosity got the better of him and he snuck out with his wee lasso and boldly entered the dark hollow. He found a frolicking baby Heffalump, Lumpy. In fear and trembling, Roo deftly threw his lasso and captured Lumpy. It wasn't long before Roo found that Lumpy was harmless and actually great fun to play with.

In an emotionally charged scene, Roo removed the lasso - 'cos a friendship's not very satisfying if you have to keep your mates tied up.

That's the second lesson.

After surviving the scary bits, it all came together when Lumpy's mother rescued Roo and everybody else realised that, just because someone looks or sounds different, it doesn't mean they're a threat.

Yep, Pooh's got it sussed. With friendship and mothers, we can save the world.

And on that note...

Las Palomas Blancas

A friend and I went out for coffee the other day.

Now, you need to understand that going out for coffee with a best woman friend is not about the coffee (although the café is carefully selected by the quality of the beverage). It's about spilling the beans, sharing your heart, and just occasionally having a whinge.

We'd both had a difficult week with the odd conflict and a couple of situations which remained unresolved. We talked up one side and down the other, making sure no stone was left unturned or problem unaired.

Finally, we fell into a comfortable silence knowing that, in many cases, acceptance is the only way forward.

As we sipped our coffee, we noticed two white doves flying under the eaves of the shop next door. Now if that's not a symbol of peace I don't know what is. As we glanced up, we read a sign hanging below the birds' perch—"Counselling and Psychotherapy Centre". My friend and I couldn't stop laughing at the synchronization of our angst and what seemed to us to be an answer straight from heaven.

I've named the two doves 'Peace' and 'Goodwill', and I hope

I can spread a little of it around. But you can't give away what you don't have.

Contentment

The author, Max Lucado, writes:

"In our world, contentment is a strange street vendor, roaming, looking for a home, but seldom finding an open door. He moves slowly from house to house, knocking on doors, offering his wares: an hour of peace, a smile of acceptance, a sigh of relief. But his goods are seldom taken. We are too busy to be content. 'Not now, thank you, I've too much to do,' we say. 'Too many marks to be made, too many achievements to be achieved.'"

I ask myself, what is it that causes this hurry sickness?

For me, I know it's a slight nervousness about tomorrow. It's like I 'must do' tomorrow today in case I lose an opportunity. So, what right do I have to steal tomorrow? Not much, I suspect when another day is not even guaranteed.

In the light of world events and natural disasters, I believe Max Lucado has a point.

"Contentment hovers everywhere. It's about taking time to care for others and to care for myself. It's a mindset, a soul-set if you will, of inner peace in chaos, of letting go of what never was, never is and never will be.

"It's a quiet process, disinterested in glory. It must be invited in; it won't break down the doors and force its way.

"Contentment doesn't scream success. And maybe that's why it's not so popular."

Contentment is defined as being at peace, with a spirit that's satisfied. It's not having our hearts seduced by the possible satisfaction of the latest gadget, relationship, or job promotion. It's being happy—whether rich or poor, whether our ship sails or comes in, or whether we win Lotto or not. It's learning to be content in whatever situation we find ourselves.

Oh, that there was somewhere we could download motivation. Maybe there is...

38

ET—Phone Home

I'm technically challenged. Often the most basic functions of my cellphone elude me. I know it can do lots of fascinating things like play music, take photos and record diary entries, but I'm too scared to try them in case it shuts down and refuses to go at all.

I do know that inside is a little card which miraculously connects my phone to my service provider, and also remembers all my contacts' details. And like my faith in God, I'd be lost without it.

Faith is like placing a SIM card in your heart. Combined with regular prayer—which could be compared to charging your spiritual batteries—faith connects me to my Provider. Unlike my Telco, I can use as many minutes as I choose. I can't prepay for all the many blessings that come my way. I can, however, sign up on a permanent plan that allows me to download love, joy, peace 24/7. My spiritual SIM card gives me a list of all those in my sphere of influence so I can be prompted to care, contact or refer them to my Provider. And in case of emergency, I know that "God help me" will always be heard.

And on that note…

I went to church a few weeks ago and the minister was in a wheelchair. It didn't take too long for me to realise that being disabled was not a handicap for this woman. She could certainly run rings around most people I know.

She told us she liked to have adventures. Frequently, she would set off in her power chair. Some of her escapades were hilarious and a bit scary. One day, she'd got a wheel stuck while trying to leap over a pavement and was left dangling precariously as her chair listed to the right. In hindsight, she said it must have looked very funny, and she was very grateful to her rescuer.

Another time, she'd ventured far from home, when the red lights on her chair battery began to blink and she realized with dismay she'd forgotten to plug her chair in to the power source the night before. She turned around and hot-wheeled it home, arriving just as the chair breathed its last gasp.

Her point was that we lead such frenetic lives and often forget that we need to charge ourselves up. To take time to play, to relax, and even to pray. To plug into a power source to keep us going and help us negotiate the bumps of life.

Three Score Years and Ten

Somebody mentioned that seventy is the maximum number of years we're promised; after that, life is a downhill spiral. That prompted me to think about what I'd learned and what might yet be ahead. I reflected on a piece I'd written a few years ago...

New Year

I'm sitting in my office; the rain is pouring down and I'm wearing winter woollies. This is summer in Auckland.

I'm tempted to feel a bit blue but then I look at 'the big picture' and see the possibilities for a brand-spanking New Year.

January is named after the Roman god, Janus. Evidently this god was able to look backwards and forwards at the same time.

Oh, that God had given that gift to mothers!

But I digress.

New Year is a good opportunity to scan the previous twelve months, to tidy up loose ends, then let go and launch into fresh challenges. I recall screwing up at times last year, so I've done a bit of soul searching. I've disappointed some people, overspent my budget, and gained weight. To be fair to myself, I've also been quite nice to a few people, given away a bit of dosh, and as for the weight—well, who really cares?

So, unlike poor old Janus who has no choice but to look back or forward, I can choose to take a wider point of view.

Sometimes a whole year can be an *annus horribilis*. Even Queen Elizabeth has had the odd one of those. There've been times when I could hardly get out of bed, let alone operate 'full-steam ahead' which is my usual way of dealing with life. But trials and tribulations are nothing new and mine will always pale in comparison to others.

I've learned a lot about myself over the last year. I've learned that I'm impatient at times and not much good at taking life lying down. I've found I'm not a very good Christian, often telling God off because he doesn't seem to honour my obvious management skills.

And therein lies the rub. I'm not 'the big cheese', the 'head honcho' or 'God's gift to mankind'. I'm just an ordinary person somewhat adrift in a boat on a stormy sea. It's not much good looking to other boaties for help, because they're trying to survive the waves just like I am. It's no good staring at the horizon hoping for salvation. The best thing I can do is set my sights on something unaffected by the storm... a lighthouse.

And that, folks, is faith.

Speaking of big cheeses ...

I love cheese. Not just any cheese. I don't like stinky cheese or processed cheese, but I'm really into brie or camembert served with pickled cucumbers, ciabatta bread, or thin water crackers.

When looking for a recipe recently I saw blazoned across the top of the cookbook, the name of a cheese company, followed by "The Cheese you can Trust". I wonder which ad boffin came up with this?

But I'm so glad they told me, because it'd be a terrible thing to deal with an untrustworthy cheese. How could I ever live a decent life if my chosen cheese was disloyal or deceitful? Why I'd never be able to hold my head high at social functions knowing the cheddar was dodgy. And those imported Stiltons and Goudas—well, you never know what they've been up to in those foreign places, what with mad cow disease and the like.

Then there's the ad campaign that reminds me 'Good things Take Time'. That one is an effective reminder for me because I find it hard to slow down, and the thought of waiting around for a few years for my cheese to mature brings a calm to my soul.

Should I ever find my cheeses wanting, I know I can fall back on my faith in God, 'cos he really is, The Big Cheese. And as the old song says, "What a Friend we have in Cheesus!"

39

Getting older brings perspective. When you're young, every success looks like a pinnacle, as though life couldn't get any better; every failure looks disastrous when not stretched out over a lifetime.

For me the best strategy I've employed is momentum. I've just kept doing something, changing tack when needed, bowing to some inevitabilities and digging my toes in when a battle was called for.

I'm a sensitive soul in some ways. I want everybody to be happy, I want to be liked and I want to be useful. But you can't please all the people all the time. My boss had a wonderful saying, "I prefer the way I'm doing it to the way you're not." People will oppose you for all sorts of reasons: jealousy, insecurity, the need to push you off your pedestal because it makes them feel better when you fall. Nevertheless, keeping on keeping on is your best plan.

I've not been the best at many things, but I've embarked on all my endeavours with grit and enthusiasm and in the end that's what got me through.

I've done some looking back but never enough to entrench

me in the past, to sully the present or to stifle the future. But sometimes, a shadow passes through my soul and I'm reminded of my failings and reconsider how I could've been a better wife, mother, or friend.

Having had two failed marriages keeps me humbled and empathic towards others. I often hear people saying that marriage is hard work, somehow implying that divorced people gave up because they couldn't put in the effort. I don't think there is anything harder to endure than a miserable marriage, and I suspect even my exes would agree.

Nobody understands more than me that I'm a force to be reckoned with. Life with me involves accommodating my "thinkies" and being challenged over unworkable and pointless behaviours. Suffering fools gladly is not my strong suit.

Sadly, I've given up on any romantic notions about relationships. The ones that seem to work best are where partners love each other with practical, down-to-earth caring and commitment. Unadulterated lust doesn't seem to provide an ideal foundation for a happy marriage. Who would've thought?

Clear as Glass

I watched a couple working together cleaning windows and they had it sussed. One cleaned the outside as the other cleaned the inside. That way they could clearly see the dirty marks which would otherwise be missed and signaled to each other as they went along. Amazingly, neither of them got their knickers in a twist when the other said, "You missed a spot."

It occurred to me then that this was the essence of a good marriage. I may not be able to see the glaring mistakes I make unless there's someone to point them out. It would help when that someone loves me dearly. Also, it's wonderful to have someone to celebrate with when you've done a good job—when you've cleaned up, so to speak. In terms of the future, two people looking at both sides can be a real plus.

I don't know about you, but I don't like cleaning windows. We lived in a two-storey house and, rather than hiring an expensive window cleaner, I tended to lean out of the windows, hanging at precarious angles, trying to reach every corner. Just when I thought I'd done a good job, and removed myself from the window ledge, slipped back inside I'd notice another, obvious smudge. It drove me nuts! And there's no point in just cleaning the outside of the window. The inside must be meticulously cleaned as well, to see a job well done.

This chore showed me a lot about myself. I could spend hundreds of dollars and heaps of time washing myself, buying expensive creams to smooth out the wrinkles (if only they worked), and I could shop 'til I drop purchasing designer clothes. These make no difference to what I am inside. I can be draped in Versace or Dior and still be grumpy, miserly and impatient.

It may take a while, but eventually people notice that our outer person doesn't match what's happening in our hearts. It's very stressful to live with that kind of conflict. And it's almost impossible to consistently display integrity if it's fake. They say that 'the eyes are the windows of our soul' and I'd like people to be able to look into mine and see what they're getting.

Before I get sucked in, assigning romance to window cleaning, I need to see through myself.

For me, the whole process of falling in love has been fraught. It's like a type of lunacy where I become unhinged and incapable of functioning on a rational level. The madness has catapulted me into making decisions I'd normally baulk at. How can someone with a reasonably high IQ and all of her marbles get carried away like that?

Even so, living without a best mate on tap is also a hard grind and I miss my illusions, singing along to Englebert Humperdink and Cliff Richard.

I'd like to think through the disadvantages of attaching emotions to people, places and things—especially to people. I'd like to give vent to my romantic urges without ending up with a person who stuffs up my life. I'd like to be dysfunctional and pathetic and fall headlong into the arms of a mature doting man.

I'd have liked to hold on to my fantasies a bit longer because relentless grappling with reality can be exhausting and needs a bolt-hole. I'd also like to blame my exes or the government or you or God or anyone else whom I perceive has been involved in my less than glittering success. But there's life to be lived and it's time to take my illusions to the second-hand shop and pass them on to someone else.

To be totally honest, I suspect they'll continue to simmer under my psyche's surface and erupt again when I least expect them. I'll never achieve the nirvana of detachment and neutrality. I'll no doubt get carried away again as I bounce off the walls of the never-ending possibilities waiting to be plucked from thin air.

I'd love a companion, someone who I could share all this with, someone who would listen and not dismiss my mental meanderings. I'd love someone to just hold my hand... oops! here I go again, humming the appropriate ABBA song.

While I'm on the subject, I'm sure George Clooney will soon tire of such a skinny wife and want me to join him in Lake Como.

40

Meanwhile, as I tottered into my eighth decade, legal issues needed to be put in place—firstly, to make a will providing funeral instructions should my plane fall out of the sky while on tour. That was straightforward enough until the lawyer asked who were to be my powers of attorney. The obvious choice was to endow the children closest at hand with this privilege, but who would be the most appropriate person to carry out my "pull the plug" instructions? Here is how the thought process worked.

One child, I suspected, may pull it too early, one wouldn't be ever able to pull it, and one would look to another for instructions. It was a bit like electing a caucus in Parliament who were not entirely happy with their portfolios. As for me, I'd be shuffling off this mortal coil and wouldn't care a bit if they all lunge for the power-source at the same time.

I heard someone wise say that we need to make old-age care plans before someone else makes them for us. I wonder if I'll be resistant to these plans when the time comes?

41

There have been two mainstays girding up my loins and multiple other parts of my personhood over many decades. The first is my faith and the second is friendships built up over a lifetime.

I have hunted down, stalked, cultivated, lassoed many people and those who have survived my efforts to befriend them have been the lights of my life. I have melancholics and sanguines, bolshie friends, gentle friends, fun friends and sensible friends.

So far, 'friends with benefits' have not been allowed into my inner circle, so to speak, although there has been the odd offer. My women friends pop up all over the place, at the end of the phone line, on my doorstep, or in my email inbox. Boy, did I need them after the break-up of my marriage! which had all the hallmarks of a really good (or bad) soap opera.

I was devastated and, unusually for me, I became depressed. It took two years before small shots of joy appeared in my beaten-up psyche.

I talked to a friend who told me that she, too, struggled to find joy in her life, despite a loving husband and stable grown children. So, we decided to take a search for joy. We would pray for it each morning and keep our eyes, ears and hearts open to it during the day.

A couple of weeks later, a new flat mate turned up with adventure in her heart and a liking for a good Pinot. My daughter, Amanda, visited from Qatar over my birthday and we talked and shopped and ate lunch at a seaside café.

The next time I was invited to my own pity party, I RSVPed, "No thanks", donned my glad rags and went out for coffee. Watch this space for joy updates.

Occasionally I've been horribly rejected by people who obviously didn't know what they were missing out on, but when I spread that disappointment over other enduring faithful friendships, it spreads very thinly. My friends have invested dearly in my life and I in theirs during distressing as well as happy times, and we now enjoy returns on that investment.

* * *

In 1776, the year of the American Declaration of Independence, a pamphlet called *Common Sense* was published. The writer was Thomas Paine and there were evidently 56 editions printed in that year alone. Thomas Paine also penned these words—"That which we obtain too easily, we esteem too lightly. It is dearness only which gives everything its value."

And maybe it's these two attitudes that stand the test of time—to have a successful, fulfilled life, we combine common sense and perseverance.

In over two hundred years, knowledge and technology have made life easier in so many ways, but I wonder what we have learned.

Each new generation has the expectation that life will be easier, money will be more readily available, and the 'slings and arrows of outrageous fortune' will not be aimed at them.

I have a few years under my belt (together with those extra pounds) and I know that life is a marathon, not a sprint. As a parent, for instance, you may feel that you have hit the wall and can't take any more. I'm here to tell you that you can take more, and more, and more.

And if you value the "dearness'", as Thomas Paine wrote, you will also enjoy the nearness of great relationships.

Don't give up, it really is worth it.

My loving God has my best interests at heart and will be there no matter what. What surprises me most is that He knows me so well and still loves me.

42

One night during a difficult time I penned this...

The Knowingness of God

It was one of those early wake-up calls, the presence of God saturating my thoughts dividing marrow from bone.

I know you, He whispered, and my heart was broken and contrite.

I sensed His knowingness. It permeated every fibre of my being. It filled my past, my present and my future. It dimmed the pain, crucified my ego, and put paid to my excuses.

I know you. You've been sought out, found out, brought out, and bought out.

I know you, when you've tried so hard and been rejected, and when you've done your share of rejecting.

I know you, when you stand in front of an audience and make them laugh and receive praise. I know you, when you bomb out, and your bubble is burst. I know you, when I cause the bones that I have broken, to rejoice and let me in with joy restored.

I know you when you stand strong in my name and resist, and I know you when tears fill a lonely night.

I know you, inside out, outside in, your upside, your down-side—when you face life head on and when you shrink beaten into little corners. I know you when you're a know-all.

My Love runs towards you when you take small bungling steps towards Me.

I let grace and mercy loose on Love's heels as well.

My knowingness catches you when you fall, straightens your path, heads off more than you can imagine.

I am your all-knowing God.

43

Miscellaneous

Eat lots of vegetables, small amounts of white bread, and moderate helpings of chocolate.

Don't complain about your weight over cheesecake and coffee with a friend.

Don't order Diet Coke with coconut cream pie. It makes you look stupid.

Clean your teeth regularly. Dentists cost a fortune and halitosis is so yesterday.

Look after your skin. It's keeping your insides in.

Exercise is necessary even if you hate it. How will you know the joy of painlessness unless you first know pain?

It is more important that wine makes your head fuzzy than that it costs a lot. Only wine snobs drink just for the taste.

Never drink alcohol two days in a row.

Never drink alone and, if desperate, don't drink two days in a row.

Give a portion of your income away and do it before you get your mitts on it. Don't ask me why that works. Maybe it's because it strikes at the root of our selfishness and gives us a bigger vision of what money's for.

Use wisdom when spending discretionary income.

Regularly check the oil and water in your car.

Write down a budget. It will keep you honest.

Always have Financial Plan "B".

See debt as the enemy.

Never tell others what you earn unless it's very small. That way they'll feel superior and may even give you stuff.

Wisdom, understanding, and knowledge are worth their weight in gold.

You can save $5 a week—you really can.

As you get older, don't learn new skills… you'll have to do more. You need to practice dumbing-down so that when going into care is necessary you will have willingly relinquished all your marbles.

Wisdom takes time and is eternally valuable; idiocy is instant and eternally costly.

Adulterers and thieves usually get caught.

Faithfulness and hard work will never let you down.

If you knew everything, you wouldn't be reading this.

Your body listens to your soul.

Don't be so far up yourself that you're irretrievable.

Be nice to your mother. When mothers die, they tell God on you.

Don't steal other peoples' food, cows, spouses, or dignity.

There is no honour among thieves; one thief always gets more of the loot.

Ask questions, even if it annoys people.

You've heard the old saying, "You made your bed, now lie in it." Make sure you have a fabulous bed and, if possible, a delicious husband to share it.

And, make your bed as soon as you get up in the morning. That way you're less likely to crawl back into it.

Laugh at yourself, with others, and for absolutely no reason but the absurdity of life.

If your life is a mess, stop moaning and change it.

Most people's dogs will bite a child, given sufficient provocation.

44

So, what about retirement, you may—or may not—ask? I have no idea, because until my body and/or mind collapse in a heap I plan to move, flat stick, until nothing functions at a normal level.

If that happens, I will drag myself across the finishing line completely drained of all my resources, shouting with glee that I left nothing unsaid, unthought, unseen or undid.

That, folks, will be my second childhood. I know I'll be trouble when the last of my marbles disengage and run under the couch. I'll be a mutterer for sure, going on and on about the multiple budgets, ideas, concepts and general craziness that have flooded my grey matter all my life. If you haven't listened to my wisdom over the years, you're going to get the lot once I've lost all my inhibitions. I'll dance like nobody's watching. Please make sure I'm clothed at all times because I don't want to traumatise anybody.

My Bucket List

Now may be the time to formally construct "My Bucket List".

My prayers and hopes are that all my children will find and

follow a workable and joy-riddled faith, that they will experience genuine happiness, and find ways to alleviate man's inhumanity and stupidity.

Can I make a difference in this world? Not in a starry, look-at-me way but by letting others know that they're not alone in their struggles; that they matter, that there is beauty for ashes, and that joy can emerge from mourning.

I'd like to end up in Cuba to somehow contribute to the lives of my friends.

I'd like to explore Turkey and France and Great Britain.

In the shredded vestiges of my fantasies, I'm sipping a prosecco at the beach in Amalfi or Venice or Greece, and across the table from me is an absolutely perfect man without spot or wrinkle and an IQ in the triple digits.

Meanwhile back in the real world, I plan to forge on, my nose to the wind, sniffing the life out of life and celebrating the fearfulness and wonderfully made-ness of all that God created me to be.

Although I'm a bit worn out and my skin bruises easily, like the Velveteen Rabbit, I know I've been loved for a long, long time. That love has given me the courage to be real.

●　●　●

And one day I will be wise, I promise.